Your
Beagle

By Dr. Robert J. Berndt

Compiled and Edited by
William W. Denlinger and R. Annabel Rathman

Cover design by
Bruce Parker

DENLINGER'S
Box 76, Fairfax, Virginia 22030

The Author, Dr. Robert J. Berndt, with the multiple Group-winning bitch Ch. Confer's Hecate.

Foreword

Your Beagle is designed as a manual for the owner of the pet Beagle as well as for those who own bench and field trial dogs. The bench Beagle and the field trial Beagle are treated separately and kennels raising these types of dogs are discussed in different chapters. This seemed a natural division since there are no longer kennels in the country today devoted to raising both types of dogs.

The advice on conditioning and grooming is based on the Author's experience as a Beagler. Modifications of such advice will have to be made from time to time to take care of the particular needs of an individual dog or line of dogs.

While it is not possible to acknowledge the help of all breeders, handlers, and judges who made suggestions for this book, the Author would like to express his gratitude to those who contributed the photographs that have been used. These photographs give a representation of Beagles, both bench and field, from all parts of the country.

I do wish to express special appreciation to Patricia E. Confer, who started me in Beagles and made it possible for me to own the Group-winning bitch, Ch. Confer's Hecate, and her daughter, Ch. RJB Harriet Confer.

R. J. B.

Contents

A litter of puppies bred by Junior's Beagles out of Ch. Junior's Belle Starr, C.D.X.

The Beagle Puppy

Charles M. Schultz, the world renowned cartoonist, has done more to popularize the Beagle than any other single individual in the United States. Everyone knows Snoopy the Beagle and his master, Charlie Brown. Snoopy has a distinct personality. He is a friend, a confidant, a sharer of joy and sadness, and one of the great folk philosophers in the world today. Snoopy never met a stranger, nor, for that matter, did his counterpart the real Beagle. Snoopy includes among his friends all the children of the neighborhood: Lucy, Peanuts, Linus, Schroeder, and the whole gang. Beagles do love children. They love people in general, but they seem to have a special affection for the rough and tumble play of the neighborhood gang.

Beagles have been extremely popular in the United States for many years. The registrations of The American Kennel Club indicate that this breed has been near the very top of the list consistently. The Beagle led the registration list in the mid-1950s but dropped to fourth place in the mid-1960s. The breed is now in third place—behind the Poodle and the German Shepherd. This popularity has been maintained because, in addition to being a good pet, the Beagle is valued by many as an excellent hunting dog.

The Beagle makes a good pet because of his size and his adaptability. Standing less than fifteen inches at the withers means that he is small enough to live comfortably in the house without taking up more than his share of space. He is adaptable to changes in environment, food, and the temperature. He can make the necessary adjustment with a minimum of effort. He is so flexible that he gives the impression at times that he is even unaware that the change required any effort on his part. He is an "easy keep" in that he seems to adjust to any diet and to get full benefit from the food. Since he is such a good eater, his diet must be watched to prevent the possibility that he will become overweight. The only quality of a Beagle that ever seems to annoy an owner is his tendency to yodel every time a squirrel or rabbit runs through the back yard.

Purchasing a family pet is an exciting event but not one that takes place every day. Since it is such an important happening, considerable planning should precede the actual purchase of the puppy. The family should take several trips to well-established breeding kennels and should attend at least one dog show to see Beagles at various stages of development from puppy to full-grown adult.

Once these preliminary steps have been taken, and the family decides to buy a Beagle, then a reputable kennel should be selected for the purchase. If there is a local kennel club and it has a kennel referral service, the problem is simplified. But many towns do not have such a service available, so it may be necessary to consult one of the national dog magazines. These magazines usually contain classified advertisements arranged in a geographical index so as to simplify finding a kennel within easy driving distance. Serious breeders, who are to be found in most localities across the country, are dedicated to the betterment of the breed and will make a great effort in helping the prospective buyer find just the right puppy.

Pet-quality Beagle puppies will cost a good deal less than show specimens, and it may be possible to find a half-grown dog even cheaper. A six-month-old dog may not be a good buy, however, for it is sometimes more difficult for the older dog to make the necessary adjustment as a family pet. That will depend to a great extent on the personality of the individual dog.

The classified section of the newspaper in larger cities will have a column advertising pets for sale. This is also a valuable source of information in looking for a kennel. Commercial pet shops usually have a wide selection of various breeds available, but owners of most pet shops do not breed their own dogs and so in turn must find breeders to supply them with their stock. Consequently, by dealing directly with a breeder a purchaser can probably save time and perhaps money.

A number of factors must be considered in selecting the individual puppy. Both female and male Beagles are good pets. Both can be trained and housebroken by the usual methods. Because males are more numerous than females, the price of males is usually lower. A lower price for males, however, would not necessarily be the case for show quality dogs.

A puppy should not be taken from his dam before he is eight weeks of age. He may be weaned by the time he is six weeks old, but the extra two weeks will give him greater stamina and more confidence when he finally does go to his new home. The puppy also has additional time to adjust to a solid food diet, and the breeder has time to have the puppy checked for worms and to be inoculated.

If there are several puppies to choose from, one has an opportunity to observe the personality of each puppy as it relates to the rest of the litter. Whether intrigued by the most aggressive and outgoing or by the most shy and retiring, a prospective buyer does get a clue to the future personality of the dog by observing puppy-play. It is certainly true that maturity and a change of home environment can modify a personality, but some of the original traits usually will remain.

By watching the puppy romp, the prospective buyer will be able to verify that he does not limp or have any other obvious physical disability. The buyer should examine the puppy to ascertain that his eyes are clear and that he has no sores or cuts on his body. Once this superficial physical examination has been completed, the buyer has an opportunity to make other rather subjective decisions—those relating to size and overall balance, for example. In many cases, though, a prospective buyer falls in love with a particular puppy and decides to buy that one without thought of the predetermined requirements he might have established. Dogs are frequently sold to buyers who make the decision on an impulse.

Before making the trip to purchase a puppy, one should make sufficient preparations for bringing him home. The simplest way to bring him home is in a cardboard box that has a lid which can be closed if he gets too nervous and tries to jump out. Several layers of newspapers should be placed in the bottom of the box and then covered by a layer of shredded newspaper or an old towel to help absorb any accidents that might result from the puppy's first car ride.

If someone will talk to him, pet him, and calm him during the drive home, the puppy will usually remain quietly in the box. Occasionally a puppy will try to climb out of the box, and if a firm, calming hand is not enough to keep him confined, closing the lid and talking to him through it will keep him where he should be. Short drives in the car later on will accustom him to riding and will make trips to the veterinarian or long drives on vacation far more pleasant for both the dog and the owner.

Just as soon as the puppy arrives at his new home, he should be allowed to romp in a fenced exercise area in the yard. This will establish, from the very first moment he is in his new home, that he is to do certain things outside. Returning him to this same place at frequent intervals, on a fixed schedule, will start the housebreaking pattern promptly and should prove most effective.

9

Within a day or two after he arrives at his new home, the puppy should be taken to the veterinarian. He will undoubtedly have been given a temporary shot by the kennel owner from whom he was purchased, but this temporary shot will only be good for a period of about two weeks. A permanent inoculation can be given when the puppy is three months old. This precaution is extremely important for the well-being of the puppy and should never be neglected.

There are three common diseases to which dogs are susceptible: distemper, hepatitis, and leptospirosis. These diseases are frequently fatal when immunization has been neglected, but there are effective inoculations against all three. The veterinarian can administer a three-in-one shot during the puppy's first visit, and at a later date he can give a booster shot. When the puppy is six months old he should also be immunized against rabies.

Long nails cause discomfort to the dog when he walks, so while the puppy is at the veterinarian's, he should have his nails clipped. The owner should learn to clip the dog's nails, for they must be clipped every week. Learning to clip the nails himself can save an owner a great deal of money over a period of time. (Instructions on nail clipping are included on page 38 of this book.) While at the veterinarian's, the dog should also have his ears checked to see that they are free from wax. He should also be checked to make sure that he is not harboring worms or other parasites.

A competent veterinarian will keep the dog in good health and keep the owner from needless care and worry. The selection of the right veterinarian is a matter that warrants serious consideration.

When the new owner purchases the puppy, the breeder will provide him with a copy of the pedigree and a blue registration certificate issued by The American Kennel Club. The registration certificate will contain all of the information required to complete the transfer of ownership from the breeder to the new owner. The certificate contains such information as the names of the sire and the dam, the date of whelping, the color and sex of the puppy, and the registration number of the litter.

The breeder must fill in certain information on the reverse side of the registration certificate in order to transfer ownership of the puppy to the new owner. The certificate must then be signed by the new owner and forwarded to The American Kennel Club together with the fee specified on the certificate.

10

Ch. Ravenswood Touch of Midas, owned by Mr. and Mrs. Donald Barnes.

The new owner will also have an opportunity to name the puppy. Two names must be submitted. The first choice will be accepted unless it has already been used for another dog.

When it is returned by The American Kennel Club, the certificate should be kept in a safe place for it represents the title of ownership of the dog. Information contained in this document will be needed if the dog is ever entered in competition at a sanctioned show, or if the dog is used for breeding.

Beagle breeder Patricia E. Confer, with (l. to r.) Ch. Confer's Hecate, Ch. RJB Harriet Confer, and Ch. Confer's Super Sandy.

Ch. Elsy's Echo of Star,
owned by Rita Randel and
W. S. Elsy

Ch. Ravenswood Passing
Fancy, owned by Mr. and
Mrs. Donald Barnes.

The Bench Beagle

The American Kennel Club recognizes only purebred dogs. It registers purebred dogs, establishes rules for the breeding of these dogs, and offers guidance to the breeders. The first step that must be taken in gaining A.K.C. recognition for a breed is to establish a Standard. The Standard, a detailed description of the breed, is the result of the efforts of the breeders who have sought the recognition of The American Kennel Club for their breed. During a period of a number of years they have maintained careful breeding records of the dogs and have acted as a semi-official registering agency for all information—including litter registrations, stud books, information pertinent to the development of the breed (such as history and evolution), and records of the importing and exporting of dogs of that breed.

At the time The American Kennel Club recognizes the breed, it formally accepts the Standard of the breed. Judges and breeders use this official description in determining the quality of the dogs.

Standards are documents difficult to prepare and to interpret. Descriptions as to size and weight present no problems, but interpreting the exact meaning may be difficult when it comes to other points. Because tastes change through the years and new breeders become active and dominant in the breed clubs, Standards are rewritten at intervals. Such evolutionary changes help to explain why breed winners in pictures dating back two or three decades appear quite different from dogs winning today.

The following is the official Standard for the Beagle adopted by The American Kennel Club.

THE STANDARD OF THE BEAGLE

Head—The skull should be fairly long, slightly domed at occiput, with cranium broad and full. *Ears*—Ears set on moderately low, long, reaching when drawn out nearly, if not quite, to the end of the nose; fine in texture, fairly broad—with almost entire absence of erectile power—setting close to the head, with the forward edge slightly inturning to the cheek—rounded at tip. *Eyes*—Eyes large, set well apart—soft and houndlike—expression gentle and pleading; of a brown or hazel color. *Muzzle*—Muzzle of medium length—straight and square-cut—the stop moderately defined. *Jaws*—Level. Lips free from flews; nostrils large and open. *Defects*—A very flat skull, narrow across the top; excess of dome, eyes small, sharp and terrier-like, or prominent and protruding; muzzle long, snipy or cut away decidedly below the eyes, or very short. Roman-nosed, or upturned, giving a dish-face expression. Ears short, set on high or with a tendency to rise above the point of origin.

Body—Neck and Throat—Neck rising free and light from the shoulders strong in substance yet not loaded, of medium length. The throat clean and free from folds of skin; a slight wrinkle below the angle of the jaw, however, may be allowable. *Defects*—A thick, short, cloddy neck carried on a line with the top of the shoulders. Throat showing dewlap and folds of skin to a degree termed "Throatiness."

Shoulders and Chest—Shoulders sloping—clean, muscular, not heavy or loaded—conveying the idea of freedom of action with activity and strength. Chest deep and broad, but not broad enough to interfere with the free play of the shoulders. *Defects*—Straight, upright shoulders. Chest disproportionately wide or with lack of depth.

Back, Loin and Ribs—Back short, muscular and strong. Loin broad and slightly arched, and the ribs well sprung, giving abundance of lung room. *Defects*—Very long or swayed or roached back. Flat, narrow loin. Flat ribs.

Forelegs and Feet—Forelegs—Straight, with plenty of bone in proportion to size of the hound. Pasterns short and straight. *Feet*—Close, round and firm. Pad full and hard. *Defects*—Out at elbows. Knees knuckled over forward, or bent backward. Forelegs crooked or Dachshund-like. Feet long, open or spreading.

Hips, Thighs, Hind Legs and Feet—Hips and thighs strong and well muscled, giving abundance of propelling power. Stifles strong and well let down. Hocks firm, symmetrical and moderately bent. Feet close and firm. *Defects*—Cowhocks, or straight hocks. Lack of muscle and propelling power. Open feet.

Tail—Set moderately high; carried gaily, but not turned forward over the back; with slight curve; short as compared with size of the hound; with brush. *Defects*—A long tail. Teapot curve or inclined forward from the root. Rat tail with absence of brush.

Coat—A close, hard, hound coat of medium length. *Defects*—A short, thin coat, or of a soft quality.

Color—Any true hound color.

General Appearance—A miniature Foxhound, solid and big for his inches, with the wear-and-tear look of the hound that can last in the chase and follow his quarry to the death.

SCALE OF POINTS

Head			Running Gear		
Skull	5		Forelegs	10	
Ears	10		Hips, thighs and		
Eyes	5		hind legs	10	
Muzzle	5	25	Feet	10	30
Body			Coat	5	
Neck	5		Stern	5	10
Chest and shoulders	15		Total	100	
Back, Loin and ribs	15	35			

Varieties—There shall be two varieties:
Thirteen Inch—which shall be for hounds not exceeding 13 inches in height.
Fifteen Inch—which shall be for hounds over 13 but not exceeding 15 inches in height.

Disqualification

Any hound measuring more than 15 inches shall be disqualified.

Approved September 10, 1957

The Standard describes an ideal Beagle. The goal of every kennel owner should be to breed to this Standard. The description is that of a sound dog that would be able to run the field for hours without tiring. The Beagle must have enough substance and muscle to carry him in this work. His chest must be of the proportion that would give sufficient wind for both running and tonguing.

Movement is important in a working Hound. Movement depends on bone and muscle and the balance between the two. A fine-boned dog with good muscle will be little better than a dog with good bone but little muscle. While both could do some field work, their stamina and staying power would be limited.

For a dog to move out, he must have good shoulder placement. If he is straight in shoulder he will not have the necessary reach to cover the ground. A dog that is straight in front usually has poor angulation in the rear, which will result in a tiring gait and further slow him. If a dog is overly angulated in the rear, he will be forced to "side-wind." That is, his back legs will overreach the stride of his front legs, and in order to avoid stepping on his own front feet, the dog will be forced to gait with his rear slightly to one side.

15

Ch. RJB Harriet Confer,
owned by the Author.

Ch. Clark's Lackawana
Tony, owned by Busch's
Beagles.

Ch. Lil Lehers Sugar and
Candy, owned by Billie R.
Huggins.

The rear is to be well muscled to give the necessary drive to the rear action of the dog. With the stifles well let down, the dog will have good reach and will be able to move smoothly through the field. If, on the other hand, the hock is too long, the gait will tend to be more uneven because the rear will have to be lifted higher to accommodate the hinge action of the back leg.

The feet are to be round and firm with the toes close together. This will afford the dog good traction on rough terrain. If the foot is splayed or the toes are spread, there is a tendency for the foot to turn, which could throw the gait out of balance.

Because of his working nature, a Beagle must be balanced in size and substance. He must in no respect be exaggerated. When a Beagle is properly set up and viewed from the side, he should give the impression of a compact little dog. He should be neither long nor short in back. There seems to be a tendency today toward a longer back. This would weaken the sustaining qualities of the Beagle in the field. On the other hand, a Beagle with an extremely short back would not be able to move with any speed or reach. While the Beagle, from chest to rear, is to be longer than he is tall, he should be just slightly so. The distance between the last rib and the front of the thigh should be moderate. The loin area should not be overly long.

The bitch is always slightly more refined than the dog. The body of the dog is heavier boned and more muscled than that of the bitch. This should be evident even when the dog is seen from a distance. A coarse-type bitch with heavy bone and excessive muscle is said to be "doggy," while a fine-boned male is "bitchy." Neither quality is desired in a breeding line.

There is a difference in the head of the dog and that of the bitch. The head of the bitch is a little more refined, is somewhat smaller, and has less muzzle. Whether it is a dog or bitch, the Beagle's head must be balanced and must be in proportion to the body.

The head is moderately broad, allowing the eyes to be set well enough apart. Large eyes set well apart will give good expression to a head of moderate breadth. If the eyes are small and set too close together, they will destroy the Hound-type expression which the Beagle must have. While the eyes are to be dark, a somewhat lighter eye is permissible in the lemon colored dog. The darker eye is still preferred, however, in any case. The eyes should be neither protruding nor sunken. A bulging eye is one that is easily injured, while a sunken one tends to tear excessively, which frequently causes other problems in the eye.

17

Ch. Gremlin's Imp of Starcrest, owned by Robert and Louise Merrill.

Multiple Best-in-Show Ch. Busch's Nuts to You of Brendons, owned by Brenda Gentry and Cecile Busch.

Ch. Lawndale's Dancing Doli, owned by John and Norma Struwe.

The skull is to be rounded but not to the extent that it could be called domed. The ear set is moderately high, but not so high that the ears are on line with the top of the skull. If they are too low, though, they give the impression that the skull is higher and more rounded than it really is. The ears should be soft and pliable and well rounded at the tips. When brought forward, the ear tips should reach almost to the end of the nose. Ears that are excessively short also tend to be very thick and coarse and will stand away from the head, giving the impression that the skull is extremely wide. Ears that are long enough to extend much beyond the tip of the nose are usually too broad and resemble those of the Bloodhound.

The muzzle is to be neither broad and square nor narrow and snipy. The bitch has slightly less breadth and depth to the muzzle than the dog. The proportion of muzzle to skull is about two to three, or the muzzle is about two-fifths the length of the entire head.

For the muzzle to have proper balance when viewed from the side, there must be a strong lower jaw. A receding lower jaw usually results in a bad bite as well as a snipy muzzle. The lower jaw must be firm enough to give a squared-off finish to the front of the muzzle.

The area under the eye should be moderately rounded, but should give no evidence of puffiness nor cheekiness. There should be evidence of flesh but no exaggeration. Complete absence of flesh in this area would give the chiseled effect of the Poodle and would cause the muzzle to be out of proportion.

The mouth of the Beagle must be strong and must have good teeth. Uneven or missing teeth are considered a fault in the ring. The scissors bite is the correct one. This puts the lower edge of the upper teeth just barely over the upper edge of the lower teeth. A good set of teeth that are evenly matched will give a firm grip and will allow no side movement when pressure is exerted from opposite directions on the upper and lower jaws.

While a breeder should mentally take his dog apart when examining him for conformation, and should realize the strengths and weaknesses of bone, muscle, and movement, he should always remember that it is the sum of the parts that determines the worth of an individual dog. It is the overall picture that the dog presents both when he is posed and when he is gaiting in the ring that determines how he will be evaluated by the judge. The individual faults will be weighed against the overall quality of a particular dog, and will be compared with similar and different faults of the other dogs in competition in determining the worth of each dog.

Field Ch. Pearson Creek Banjo, owned by the George Nixons.

Field Ch. Pearson Creek Stub, owned by the George Nixons.

Ravenswood Beagles running a rabbit.

The Field Trial Beagle

The Beagle is unique among all breeds of dogs in the United States for he is one of the few dogs that still functions as a working dog for the purpose for which he was bred. It is true that there are dogs of other breeds still performing the work for which they were created, but in no other breed is the percentage of true working dogs as high as in the case of the Beagle. While the degree of training and performance may vary greatly among individual specimens, there is a high consistency of participation.

While the field trial Beagle may not always be a thing of beauty when compared to the bench type dog, he certainly is a joy to behold when he is on the scent following his quarry—whether it be rabbit, bird, or fox. The picture of the running Beagle brings admiration even from the uninitiated in the breed.

The field type Beagle today differs somewhat more from his bench counterpart than he did in the past. This is evidenced by the fact that it has been many years since there was a dual champion that earned titles both as a field dog and as a bench dog. This difference has undoubtedly been created unconsciously by those kennels that breed bench type exclusively and have no interest in the field aspects of the breed.

When comparing a bench dog and a field dog standing side by side, it is easy to see that they are the same breed, but it is also evident that there is a difference. The field Beagle is a more compact, more solid dog and gives the impression that he is somewhat shorter on leg. The bench Beagle is a sleeker, rangier type with a more elegant appearance. He stands somewhat taller on leg and usually has neither the depth nor the breadth of chest. This has led many field trial men to turn away from the bench dog, for they feel that bench dogs do not have the stamina necessary to run rabbits all day long. Bench men are usually very reluctant to take their dogs to field for fear of the dogs' receiving an injury that would disqualify them in the ring. This debate will continue until there is sufficient interest and energy to produce dual champions again.

It is the selective breeding process of both types of Beagles that has produced the present-day dogs. With the field dog, shortness

21

Ch. Wright-Eager Lady's Minute Man, owned by the Charles Wrights.

of leg and compactness of body are definite advantages when trying to get under low shrubs and bushes to flush out game. Breadth and depth of chest mean good wind which contributes to stamina and staying power. By the consistent selection of dogs of this type for a breeding program, a uniform dog can be bred that will continue to reproduce his self-type through succeeding generations.

In addition to these physical qualities, a Beagle must also have certain psychological qualities. These again can be bred into a line through a selective breeding program. The Beagle must be intense when he is running in the field. He must have a single purpose in mind while on scent and must not be distracted from his goal. Many breeders consider this trait an instinct or a pre-taught characteristic of certain lines.

Because the Beagle is a "Scent Hound" rather than a "Sight Hound," he must have a good nose—one that can easily distinguish one scent from among several. He must be able to follow this scent to his quarry. In addition to having a good nose, he must also have a good throat, one that is well open and capable of producing a good strong voice. Not only must he have a good voice, but also he must know how and when to use it. He should tongue, or sing, or yodel, only when moving on the scent. The voice should be clear and deep and of a carrying quality.

The field dog begins his training while still a puppy. The average age for starting this training is between three and four months.

Ch. Elsy's Painted Lady, owned by W. S. Elsy.

Ch. Wright-Eager Gold Nugget, owned by the Charles Wrights.

The dog is usually tested for natural hunting habits or pre-taught qualities before formal training is begun. Since each dog must be trained individually, it is only wise to find out what strengths the dog already has. Once the natural ability of a dog has been determined, his training can be started.

The dog is started slowly and gently to give him confidence and to avoid any possible confusion that strange surroundings might cause. The first time he is taken to field, he may go alone with his trainer or with an older, trained Beagle that is to share in the training. It is extremely important when using an older dog to train a puppy that he be a well-trained dog that has no faults in method or action. If the older dog has such faults, the puppy will pick them up. It is ironic that Beagles seem to have a talent to pick up the bad habits faster than they pick up the good habits.

The regularity of training sessions is of great importance. The regularity of these sessions is more important than the length of each one. The pattern of performing, being corrected, and then reperforming on a regular schedule is what locks the habit and makes it a conditioned response to given stimuli. If a regular schedule is not maintained, the dog must face each situation and think it out rather than reacting automatically to it.

The trainer must be firm with the dog and consistent in his level of expectation for the performance of the dog. He must not vary levels of expected behavior from day to day or he will confuse the

Ch. Hoss Enpeffer, owned by Marvan Kennels.

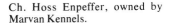

Ch. Wright-Eager Hardy Boy (left), owned by the Charles Wrights, and Ch. Ridge-land's Tuff Guy, owned by Harlan Cannon and Damaris Wright.

Ch. Fulmont's Fable, owned by the William Fulkersons.

dog. This consistency on the part of the handler is a great kindness to the dog.

The dog must be taught a limited number of commands so that the handler will easily be able to work him in the field with a minimum of talk. He must learn to pick up a scent, follow it to the game, flush the animal, and then pursue the quarry. He must be determined and steady in his actions while performing these specific steps. Once the Beagle has been trained, there is the challenge of entering him in competition at a field trial.

The first field trial was held in Massachusetts in 1890 and was sponsored by the National Beagle Club. Today there are between four and five hundred approved trials each year, so there is plenty of opportunity to test a Beagle once it has been thoroughly trained.

While Beagles are usually entered in individual competition, there are still trials for packs. In the United States today there are fewer than twenty registered packs. The training of these dogs differs somewhat from the training of an individual dog. In a pack each dog must be cooperative and must work as a part of a larger unit. These dogs are trained to perform to the command of a horn and the dogs are usually run with the handlers on horseback rather than on foot.

The American Kennel Club approved the following Standard for packs in 1957.

PACKS OF BEAGLES

Score of Points for Judging

Hounds—General Levelness of pack	40%	
Individual merit of hounds	30%	
		70%
Manners		20%
Appointments		10%
		100%

Levelness of Pack—The first thing in a pack to be considered is that they present a unified appearance. The hounds must be as near to the same height, weight, conformation and color as possible.

Individual Merit of the Hounds—Is the individual bench-show quality of the hounds. A very level and sporty pack can be gotten together and not a single hound be a good Beagle. This is to be avoided.

Manners—The hounds must all work gaily and cheerfully, with flags up—obeying all commands cheerfully. They should be broken to heel up, kennel up, follow promptly and stand. Cringing, sulking, lying down to be avoided. Also, a pack must not work as though in terror of master and whips. In Beagle packs it is recommended that the whip be used as little as possible.

Appointments—Master and whips should be dressed alike, the master or huntsman to carry horn—the whips and master to carry light thong whips. One whip should carry extra couplings on shoulder strap.

Ch. Mitzi Jo of the Merry Beagles, owned by Charles Hall.

Ch. Golden Trinket of Starcrest, owned by Diana L. Allen and Louise C. Merrill.

Ch. Busch's Bonnie Prince Charlie, owned by William and Cecile Busch.

Recommendations for Show Livery

Black velvet cap, white stock, green coat, white breeches or knickerbockers, green or black stockings, white spats, black or dark brown shoes. Vest and gloves optional. Ladies should turn out exactly the same except for a white skirt instead of white breeches.

Approved September 10, 1957

There are three types of trials for individual Beagles: an A Sanction, a B Sanction, and a Licensed Trial. The A Trial lasts two days while the B Trial lasts but one day. Neither of these will produce points leading to the title of field champion. It is only the Licensed Trial, which lasts four days, that produces the necessary points.

To earn the title of field trial champion, a dog must earn a total of 120 points and must win three First Place awards. There are two judges at each trial who will score the dogs on a comparative basis, using a scale of 100 points. The dogs are run in braces with the winners of each of the first five top braces being brought back to run in a second series. If the winners cannot be determined from a second series, other series may be run. The final placements are selective in that each dog will have defeated the dog placed behind him, and will have been defeated by the one placed ahead of him. The dog winning First will receive one point for each dog in competition. The Second Place dog will receive half this number, the Third Place dog one-third, and the Fourth Place dog one-fourth. The Fifth Place dog will be given Reserve.

The Beagles are divided by sex and height, thus giving two classes for thirteen inch and two for fifteen inch dogs. A drawing is held to determine the brace mate for this first series. These same dogs will not run against each other a second time during the trial.

There are special age classifications which can earn the title of Derby or Futurity winner. Derby competition is limited to the calendar year in which the dog is whelped and to the following calendar year. Futurity competition is limited to the first calendar year after a dog passes the limit for the Derby. These added titles carry special honors.

The title of field champion is one that should be highly respected because of the special significance it carries. The title indicates that the Beagle is a sound dog capable of working the field. It also indicates that the trainer and handler are knowledgeable about the breed and that they have dedicated themselves to the time-consuming training of these quality dogs.

Ch. Ravenswood Softwalker, owned by Mr. and Mrs. Donald Barnes.

Conditioning the Beagle

The conditioning of the Beagle is of prime importance both for his health and for his happiness. The key to proper conditioning is the basic diet of the dog, so a well-balanced diet should be maintained at all times. Meals can be varied to make them interesting without sacrificing standards of nutrition, and vitamin and mineral supplements can be added.

A dog cannot grow the correct coat unless he is fed a well-balanced diet. To produce such a coat, a Beagle must gain and must maintain the weight consistent with his size. Although an overly fat dog may be accepted as a family pet, he cannot be accepted as a show dog. Because a Beagle quickly becomes overweight if given an opportunity to overeat, his food must be measured. The quantity of food can be increased with increased exercise, but the dog's weight should be checked at regular intervals to prevent unwanted gains.

Proper exercise is necessary for all dogs, so an hour or two each day should be set aside to exercise the dog. With a family pet this can be accomplished by allowing the dog to romp in a fenced area, or by taking the dog for a walk. A well-drained run covered with three or four inches of gravel will keep the dog out of the mud on rainy days. An occasional treatment with lime eliminates odors from the run. Dry lime can be sprinkled over the surface and then washed through thoroughly with a hose to prevent the dog's picking it up on his feet.

To stay in top shape and to maintain the correct muscle tone, Beagles need more exercise than many other breeds. When Beagles are allowed to run in groups in a large fenced area, they are able to get the necessary exercise. However, when a Beagle is alone he will need some road work to maintain muscle tone.

One of the techniques that Beagle owners use is to lead the dog while riding a bicycle. Depending on the need of the particular dog, the run can be from three to five miles a day and at a pace that the dog would use while working in the field. If there is more than one dog that needs this type of training, another method can be used. Several dogs can be led from the tailgate of a station wagon.

Great care will have to be used to maintain control of the dogs. The use of double leads, one set tied together, should protect against a dog's getting away.

Regulated exercise is important not only for the field trial dog, but also for the bench Beagle. A dog that is underexercised will not gait properly and cannot possibly maintain the necessary balance of muscle to bone. A carefully structured training program should be established and adhered to in order to keep the Beagle in prime condition.

Bench Beagles should be trained in show ring pattern drills while they are still very young so that this will become a part of their routine. They should be taught the correct show pose and trained to hold the pose for the proper length of time. Since the attention span of some Beagles in the ring is short, they will have to be trained over a long enough period of time so that they can develop the necessary self-discipline to stand for the examination of the judge.

When the puppy is just a few weeks old he should be set up in a show pose. The feet should be correctly placed so that the puppy gets the feel of this position. Should the puppy move his feet, they should be reset with a gentle but firm action. The foot is set by grasping the leg above the elbow joint, which permits the trainer to control not only the motion of the foot but of the whole leg. The dog will then be in a firm, comfortable position that could not be achieved by merely twisting the foot. If the foot is not solidly placed, the dog will lean for balance—which will not be to his advantage.

The angulation of the rear should be moderate. The hocks are not perpendicular to the floor, but rather extend slightly to the rear. Holding the stern just above the base will keep it erect. The head can be held in the proper position with the lead if the dog is well trained and patient. If this is not the case, the head can be held properly in position from the side away from the judge. With three fingers under the jaw and the thumb on the cheek, the handler can easily steady the head and hold it in position. He will have good control of the dog with one hand on the tail regulating the rear and the other on the head.

While field trial Beagles are usually not trimmed, bench type Beagles are. Unless a dog has an extremely sparse coat, he will require some scissoring and some clipping. The trimming is not extensive and is not designed to alter the dog. The purpose is to make the dog look neat and more finished. This may not be as important in breed competition, but it is definitely an advantage in the Group.

The clippers with a Number 10 blade are used on the throat and the front of the chest. The area covered will be from the back of the jaw down to the top of the brisket. The side lines are defined by the ridge of hair that is formed where the side coat changes growth direction when it meets the chest hair. The rear of the dog is clipped between the hair growth ridges on the back of the thighs down to the curve between the legs. These ridge areas on both the chest and the rear should then be trimmed down with the thinning shears so that the hair lies smooth and flat against the body. This cosmetic scissoring will allow the judge to see the real outline of the dog rather than the deceptive outline that would be created by excessive coat.

Clippers are also used on the rear of the hocks and the rear of the pasterns, for the hair seems to grow more than is necessary in these areas. The foot hair is trimmed even with the edge of the pads and to the root of the nail. The hair is also trimmed from between the pads to increase the footing of the dog as it gaits in the ring. Nails are trimmed weekly and kept as short as possible.

The edge of the ears may need a little evening-up of any extra long hairs that would destroy the outline. The hair around the ear opening itself tends to grow in several directions and may prevent the ear from lying flat against the head. Thinning this excessive or unruly hair improves the appearance of the ear set.

The whiskers and the eyebrows should be trimmed even with the skin. Beagles seem to have a knack for pulling in their whiskers during trimming. Sliding the finger under the lip helps hold the whiskers out and facilitates cutting them.

The feet of the Beagle are usually chalked when the dog is in competition. Chalk rubbed into the white hair will serve as a dry-cleaning agent and will absorb any oil that has accumulated since the bath the day before the show. After the chalk has been in the coat a few minutes it should be brushed out thoroughly.

The final step in readying the dog for the ring is to spray the coat with coat dressing and rub it dry with either a grooming mitt or a bristle brush.

Ch. Junior's Belle Starr, C.D.X., owned by Dick Johnson.

Ch. Ridgeland Bugle Bugs, owned by Harlan Cannon.

Multiple Best-in-Show and Specialty winner Ch. Kings Creek Triple Threat, owned by Tom and Marcia Foy.

Grooming and General Coat Care

Although coat types, textures, and patterns may seem purely arbitrary matters of little consequence, they are among the important characteristics that distinguish one breed from another. Actually, each breed has been developed to serve a specific purpose, and the coat that is considered typical for the breed is also the one most appropriate for the dog's specialized use—be it as guard, hunting companion, herder, or pet. A knowledge of the breed Standard approved by The American Kennel Club is helpful to the owner who takes pride in owning a well-groomed dog, typical of its breed.

Dogs with short, smooth coats (such as the Weimaraner, Basset, Beagle, smooth Dachshund and Chihuahua) usually shed only moderately and their coats require little routine grooming other than thorough brushing with a bristle brush or hound glove. For exhibition in the show ring, the whiskers, or "feelers," are trimmed close to the muzzle, but no other trimming is needed.

The wire coat of the Airedale, Wire Fox Terrier, Miniature Schnauzer, or Wirehaired Dachshund should be stripped or plucked in show trim at regular intervals. The dog can then be kept well groomed by thorough combing and brushing.

Curly coated breeds such as the Curly Coated Retriever, and the American and Irish Water Spaniels, generally require no special coat care other than frequent brushing. True curly coated breeds are very curly indeed and are not to be confused with breeds such as the Golden Retriever, Gordon Setter, Brittany Spaniel, and English Springer Spaniel, which have slightly curled or wavy coats of somewhat silky texture. The longer hair, or "feathers," typically found on tail, legs, ears, and chest of these breeds should be trimmed slightly to make the outline neater.

33

(UPPER LEFT) Wire brush (RIGHT) Bristle brush
(LOWER LEFT) Comb—Hound glove.

They are not "trimmed to pattern," however, as are such long-haired breeds as the Kerry Blue Terrier and the Poodle, which, when shown in the breed ring, must be clipped and trimmed in the patterns specified in the breed Standards.

The Longhaired Dachshund, the Borzoi, and the Yorkshire Terrier have long but comparatively silky coats, whereas the Newfoundland and the Rough Collie have long straight coats with rather harsh texture. Long coats must be kept brushed out thoroughly to eliminate mats and snarls.

The dog should be taught from puppyhood that a grooming session is a time for business, not for play. He should be handled gently, though, for it is essential to avoid hurting him in any way. Grooming time should be pleasant for both dog and master.

Tools required vary with the breed, but always include combs, brushes, and nail clippers and files. Combs should have wide-spaced teeth with rounded ends so that the dog's skin will not be scratched accidentally. For the same reason, brushes with natural bristles are usually preferable to those with synthetic bristles that may be too fine and sharp.

A light, airy, pleasant place in which to work is desirable, and it is of the utmost importance that neither dog nor master be distracted by other dogs, cats, or people. Consequently, it is usually preferable that grooming be done indoors.

Particularly for large or medium breeds, a sturdy grooming table is desirable. Many owners hold small puppies or Toy dogs during grooming sessions, athough it is better if they, too, are groomed on a table. Large and medium size dogs should be taught to jump onto the table and to jump off again when grooming is completed. Small dogs must be lifted on and off to avoid falls and possible injury. The dog should stand while the back and upper portions of the body are groomed, and lie on his side while underparts of his body are brushed, nails clipped, etc.

Before each session, the dog should be permitted to relieve himself. Once grooming is begun, it is important to avoid keeping the dog standing so long that he becomes tired. If a good deal of grooming is needed, it should be done in two or more short periods.

It is almost impossible to brush too much, and show dogs are often brushed for a full half hour a day, year round. If you cannot brush your dog every day, you should brush him a minimum of two or three times a week. Brushing removes loose skin particles and stimulates circulation, thereby improving condition of the skin. It also stimulates secretion of the natural skin oils that make the coat look healthy and beautiful.

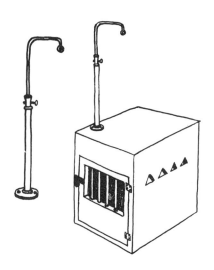

Dog crate with grooming—table top is ideal—providing rigid, well supported surface on which to groom dog, and serving as indoor kennel for puppy or grown dog. Rubber matting provides non-slip surface. Dog's collar may be attached to adjustable arm. Light-weight and readily transported yet sturdy, the crate is especially useful to owner who takes dog with him when he travels.

Before brushing, any burs adhering to the coat, as well as matted hair, should be carefully removed, using the fingers and coarse toothed comb with a gentle, teasing motion to avoid tearing the coat. The coat should first be brushed lightly in the direction in which the hair grows. Next, it should be brushed vigorously in the opposite direction, a small portion at a time, making sure the bristles penetrate the hair to the skin, until the entire coat has been brushed thoroughly and all loose soil removed. Then the coat should be brushed in the direction the hair grows, until every hair is sleekly in place.

The dog that is kept well brushed needs bathing only rarely. Once or twice a year is usually enough. Except for unusual circumstances when his coat becomes excessively soiled, no puppy under six months of age should be bathed in water. If it is necessary to bathe a puppy, extreme care must be exercised so that he will not become chilled. No dog should be bathed during cold weather and then permitted to go outside immediately. Whatever the weather, the dog should always be given a good run outdoors and permitted to relieve himself before he is bathed.

Various types of "dry baths" are available at pet supply stores. In general, they are quite satisfactory when circumstances are such that a bath in water is impractical. Dry shampoos are usually rubbed into the dog's coat thoroughly, then removed by vigorous towelling or brushing.

Before starting a water bath, the necessary equipment should be assembled. This includes a tub of appropriate size, and another tub or pail for rinse water. (A small hose with a spray nozzle—one that may be attached to the water faucet—is ideal for rinsing the dog.) A metal or plastic cup for dipping water, special dog shampoo, a small bottle of mineral or olive oil, and a supply of absorbent cotton should be placed nearby, as well as a supply of heavy towels, a wash cloth, and the dog's combs and brushes.

The amount of water required will vary according to the size of the dog, but should reach no higher than the dog's elbows. Bath water and rinse water should be slightly warmer than lukewarm, but should not be hot.

To avoid accidentally getting water in the dog's ears, place a small amount of absorbent cotton in each. With the dog standing in the tub, wet his body by using the cup to pour water over him. Take care to avoid wetting the head, and be careful to avoid getting water or shampoo in the eyes. (If you should accidentally do so, placing a few drops of mineral or olive oil in the inner corner of the eye will bring relief.) When the dog is thoroughly wet, put a small amount of shampoo on his back and work up a lather, rubbing briskly. Wash his entire body and then rinse as much of the shampoo as possible from the coat by dipping water from the tub and pouring it over the dog.

Dip the wash cloth into clean water, wring it out enough so it won't drip, then wash the dog's head, taking care to avoid the eyes. Remove the cotton from the dog's ears and sponge them gently, inside and out. Shampoo should never be used inside the ears, so if they are extremely soiled, sponge them clean with cotton saturated with mineral or olive oil. (Between baths, the ears should be cleaned frequently in the same way.)

Replace the cotton in the ears, then use the cup and container of rinse water (or hose and spray nozzle) to rinse the dog thoroughly. Quickly wrap a towel around him, remove him from the tub, and towel him as dry as possible. To avoid getting an impromptu bath yourself, you must act quickly, for once he is out of the tub, the dog will instinctively shake himself.

While the hair is still slightly damp, use a clean comb or brush to remove any tangles. If the hair is allowed to dry first, it may be completely impossible to remove them.

So far as routine grooming is concerned, the dog's eyes require little attention. Some dogs have a slight accumulation of mucus in the corner of the eyes upon waking mornings. A salt solution (1 teaspoon of table salt to one pint of warm, sterile water) can be sponged around the eyes to remove the stain. During grooming sessions it is well to inspect the eyes, since many breeds are prone to eye injury. Eye problems of a minor nature may be treated at home (see page 50), but it is imperative that any serious eye abnormality be called to the attention of the veterinarian immediately.

Feeding hard dog biscuits and hard bones helps to keep tooth surfaces clean. Slight discoloration may be readily removed by rubbing with a damp cloth dipped in salt or baking soda. The dog's head should be held firmly, the lips pulled apart gently, and the teeth rubbed lightly with the dampened cloth. Regular

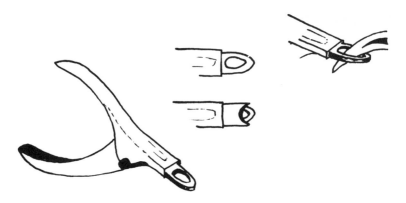

Nail trimmer—center detail shows blade cutting action. Right shows manner of inserting nail in cutter.

care usually keeps the teeth in good condition, but if tartar accumulates, it should be removed by a veterinarian.

If the dog doesn't keep his nails worn down through regular exercise on hard surfaces, they must be trimmed at intervals, for nails that are too long may cause the foot to spread and thus spoil the dog's gait. Neglected nails may even grow so long that they will grow into a circle and puncture the dog's skin. Nails can be cut easily with a nail trimmer that slides over the nail end. The cut is made just outside the faintly pink bloodline that can be seen on white nails. In pigmented nails, the bloodline is not easily seen, so the cut should be made just outside the hooklike projection on the underside of the nails. A few downward strokes with a nail file will smooth the cut surface, and, once shortened, nails can be kept short by filing at regular intervals.

Care must be taken that nails are not cut too short, since blood vessels may be accidentally severed. Should you accidentally cut a nail so short that it bleeds, apply a mild antiseptic and keep the dog quiet until bleeding stops. Usually, only a few drops of blood will be lost. But once a dog's nails have been cut painfully short, he will usually object when his feet are handled.

Nutrition

The main food elements required by dogs are proteins, fats, and carbohydrates. Vitamins A, B complex, D, and E are essential, as are ample amounts of calcium and iron. Nine other minerals are required in small amounts but are amply provided in almost any diet, so there is no need to be concerned about them. The most important nutrient is protein and it must be provided every day of the dog's life, for it is essential for normal daily growth and replacement of body tissues burned up in daily activity. Preferred animal protein products are beef, mutton, horse meat, and boned fish. Visceral organs—heart, liver, and tripe—are good but if used in too large quantities may cause diarrhea (bones in large amounts have the same effect). Pork, particularly fat pork, is undesirable. The "meat meal" used in some commercial foods is made from scrap meat processed at high temperatures and then dried. It is not quite so nutritious as fresh meat, but in combination with other protein products, it is an acceptable ingredient in the dog's diet.

Cooked eggs and raw egg yolk are good sources of protein, but raw egg white should never be fed since it cannot be digested by the dog and may cause diarrhea. Cottage cheese and milk (fresh, dried, and canned) are high in protein, also. Puppies thrive on milk and it can well be included in the diet of older dogs, too, if mixed with meat, vegetables, and meal. Soy-bean meal, wheat germ meal, and dried brewers yeast are vegetable products high in protein and may be used to advantage in the diet.

Vegetable and animal fats in moderate amounts should be used, especially if a main ingredient of the diet is dry or kibbled food. Fats should not be used excessively or the dog may become overweight. Generally, fats should be increased slightly in the winter and reduced somewhat during warm weather.

Carbohydrates are required for proper assimilation of fats. Dog biscuits, kibble, dog meal, and other dehydrated foods are good sources of carbohydrates, as are cereal products derived from rice, corn, wheat, and ground or rolled oats.

Vegetables supply additional proteins, vitamins, and minerals, and by providing bulk are of value in overcoming constipation. Raw or cooked carrots, celery, lettuce, beets, asparagus, tomatoes, and cooked spinach may be used. They should always be chopped or ground well and mixed with the other food. Various combinations may be used, but a good home-mixed ration for the mature dog consists of two parts of meat and one each of vegetables and dog meal (or cereal product).

Dicalcium phosphate and cod-liver oil are added to puppy diets to ensure inclusion of adequate amounts of calcium and Vitamins A and D. Indiscriminate use of dietary supplements is not only unjustified but may actually be harmful and many breeders feel that their over-use in diets of extremely small breeds may lead to excessive growth as well as to overweight at maturity.

Foods manufactured by well-known and reputable food processors are nutritionally sound and are offered in sufficient variety of flavors, textures, and consistencies that most dogs will find them tempting and satisfying. Canned foods are usually "ready to eat," while dehydrated foods in the form of kibble, meal, or biscuits may require the addition of water or milk. Dried foods containing fat sometimes become rancid, so to avoid an unpalatable change in flavor, the manufacturer may not include fat in dried food but recommend its addition at the time the water or milk is added.

Candy and other sweets are taboo, for the dog has no nutritional need for them and if he is permitted to eat them, he will usually eat less of foods he requires. Also taboo are fried foods, highly seasoned foods and extremely starchy foods, for the dog's digestive tract is not equipped to handle them.

Frozen foods should be thawed completely and warmed at least to lukewarm, while hot foods should be cooled to lukewarm. Food should be in a fairly firm state, for sloppy food is difficult for the dog to digest.

Whether meat is raw or cooked makes little difference, so long as the dog is also given the juice that seeps from the meat during cooking. Bones provide little nourishment, although gnawing bones helps make the teeth strong and helps to keep tartar from accumulating on them. Beef bones, especially large knuckle bones, are best. Fish, poultry, and chop bones should never be given to dogs since they have a tendency to splinter and may puncture the dog's digestive tract.

Clean, fresh, cool water is essential to all dogs and an adequate supply should be readily available twenty-four hours a day from the time the puppy is big enough to walk. Especially during hot weather, the drinking pan should be emptied and refilled at frequent intervals.

Puppies usually are weaned by the time they are six weeks old, so when you acquire a new puppy ten to twelve weeks old, he will already have been started on a feeding schedule. The breeder should supply exact details as to number of meals per day, types and amounts of food offered, etc. It is essential to adhere to this established routine, for drastic changes in diet may produce intestinal upsets.

Until a puppy is six months old, milk formula is an integral part of the diet. A day's supply should be made up at one time and stored in the refrigerator, and the quantity needed for each meal warmed at feeding time. The following combination is good for all breeds:

| 1 pint whole fresh milk | 1 tablespoon lime water |
| 1 raw egg yolk, slightly beaten | 1 tablespoon lactose |

The two latter items (as well as cod-liver oil and dicalcium phosphate to be added to solid food) are readily available at pet supply stores and drug stores.

At twelve weeks of age the amount of formula given at each feeding will vary from three to four tablespoonfuls for the Toy breeds, to perhaps two cupfuls for the large breeds. If the puppy is on the five-meal-a-day schedule when he leaves the kennel, three of the meals (first, third, and fifth each day) should consist of formula only. On a four-meal schedule, the first and fourth meals should be formula.

In either case, the second meal of the day should consist of chopped beef (preferably raw). The amount needed will vary from about three tablespoonfuls for Toy breeds up to one-half cupful for large breeds. The other meal should consist of equal parts of chopped beef and strained, cooked vegetables to which is added a little dry toast. (If you plan eventually to feed your dog canned food or dog meal, it can gradually be introduced at this meal.) Cod-liver oil and dicalcium phosphate should be mixed with the food for this meal. The amount of each will vary from one-half teaspoonful for Toys to 1 tablespoonful for large breeds.

The amount of food offered at each meal must gradually be increased and by five months the puppy will require about twice what he needed at three months. Puppies should be fat, and it is best to let them eat as much as they want at each meal, so long as they are hungry again when it is time for the next feeding. Any food not eaten within fifteen minutes should be taken away. With a little attention to the dog's eating habits, the owner can prepare enough food and still not waste any.

When the puppy is five months old, the final feeding of the day can be eliminated and the five meals compressed into four so the puppy still receives the same quantities and types of food. At six or seven months, the four meals can be compressed into three. By the time a puppy of small or medium breed is eleven to twelve months old, feedings can be reduced to two meals a day. At the end of the first year, cod-liver oil and dicalcium phosphate can usually be discontinued.

Large breeds mature more slowly and three meals a day are usually necessary until eighteen or twenty-four months of age. Cod-liver oil and dicalcium phosphate should be continued, too, until the large dog reaches maturity.

A mature dog usually eats slightly less than he did as a growing puppy. For mature dogs, one large meal a day is usually sufficient, although some owners prefer to give two meals. As long as the dog enjoys optimum health and is neither too fat nor too thin, the number of meals a day makes little difference.

The amount of food required for mature dogs will vary. With canned dog food or home-prepared foods (that is, the combination of meat, vegetables, and meal), the approximate amount required is one-half ounce of food per pound of body weight. Thus, about eight ounces of such foods would be needed each day for a mature dog weighing sixteen pounds. If the dog is fed a dehydrated commercial food, approximately one ounce of food is needed for each pound of body weight. Approximately one pound of dry food per day would be required by a dog weighing sixteen pounds. Most manufacturers of commercial foods provide information on packages as to approximate daily needs of various breeds.

As a dog becomes older and less active, he may become too fat. Or his appetite may decrease so he becomes too thin. It is necessary to adjust the diet in either case, for the dog will live longer and enjoy better health if he is maintained in trim condition. The simplest way to decrease or increase body weight is by decreasing or increasing the amount of fat in the diet. Protein content should be maintained at a high level throughout the dog's life, although the amount of food at each meal can be decreased if the dog becomes too fat.

If the older dog becomes reluctant to eat, it may be necessary to coax him with special food he normally relishes. Warming the food will increase its aroma and usually will help to entice the dog to eat. If he still refuses, rubbing some of the food on the dog's lips and gums may stimulate interest. It may be helpful also to offer food in smaller amounts and increase the number of meals per day. Foods that are highly nutritious and easily digested are especially desirable for older dogs. Small amounts of cooked, ground liver, cottage cheese, or mashed, hard-cooked eggs should be included in the diet often.

Before a bitch is bred, her owner should make sure that she is in optimum condition—slightly on the lean side rather than fat. The bitch in whelp is given much the same diet she was fed prior to breeding, with slight increases in amounts of meat, liver, and dairy products. Beginning about six weeks after breeding, she should be fed two meals per day rather than one, and the total daily intake increased. (Some bitches in whelp require as much as 50% more food than they consume normally.) She must not be permitted to become fat, for whelping problems are more likely to occur in overweight dogs. Cod-liver oil and dicalcium phosphate should be provided until after the puppies are weaned. The amount of each will vary from one-half teaspoonful to one tablespoonful a day, depending upon her size.

The dog used only occasionally for breeding will not require a special diet, but he should be well fed and maintained in optimum condition. A dog that is at public stud and used frequently may require a slightly increased amount of food. But his basic diet will require no change so long as his general health is good and his flesh is firm and hard.

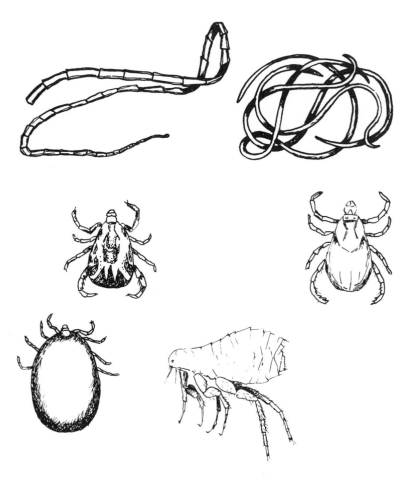

Some common internal and external parasites.

(UPPER LEFT) Tape worm. (UPPER RIGHT) Round worms. (CENTER) American dog ticks—left, female and right, male (much enlarged). (LOWER LEFT) Female tick engorged. (LOWER RIGHT) dog flea (much enlarged).

Maintaining the
Dog's Health

Proper nutrition is essential in maintaining the dog's resistance to infectious diseases, in reducing susceptibility to organic diseases, and, of course, in preventing dietary deficiency diseases. *Rickets* is probably the most common deficiency disease and afflicts puppies not provided sufficient calcium and Vitamin D. Bones fail to calcify properly, development of teeth is retarded, joints become knobby and deformed, and muscles are flabby. Symptoms include lameness, arching of neck and back, and a tendency of the legs to bow. Treatment consists of providing adequate amounts of dicalcium phosphate and Vitamin D and exposing the dog to sunlight. If detected and treated before reaching an advanced stage, bone damage may be lessened somewhat, although it cannot be corrected completely.

Osteomalacia, similar to rickets, may occur in adult dogs. Treatment is the same as for rickets, but here, too, prevention is preferable to cure. Permanent deformities resulting from rickets or osteomalacia will not be inherited, so once victims recover, they can be used for breeding.

To prevent the growth of disease-producing bacteria and other micro-organisms, cleanliness is essential. All equipment, especially water and food dishes, must be kept immaculately clean. Cleanliness is also essential in controlling external parasites, which thrive in unsanitary surroundings.

Fleas, lice, mites, and ticks can be eradicated in the dog's quarters by regular use of one of the insecticide sprays with a four to six weeks' residual effect. Bedding, blankets, and pillows should be laundered frequently and treated with an insecticide containing rotenone or DDT. Treatment for external parasites varies, depending upon the parasite involved, but a number of good dips and powders are available at pet stores.

Fleas may be eliminated by using a flea powder containing lindane. The coat must be dusted thoroughly with the powder at frequent intervals during the summer months when fleas are a problem. For eradicating lice, dips containing rotenone or DDT must be applied to the coat. A fine-toothed comb should then be used to remove dead lice and eggs, which are firmly attached to the coat. Mites live deep in the ear canal, producing irritation to the lining of the ear and causing a brownish-black, dry type discharge. Plain mineral oil or ear ointment should be swabbed on the inner surface of the ear twice a week until mites are eliminated. Ticks may carry Rocky Mountain spotted fever, so, to avoid possible infection, they should be removed from the dog only with tweezers and should be destroyed by burning (or by dropping them into insecticide). Heavy infestation can be controlled by sponging the coat daily with a solution containing a special tick dip.

Among preparations available for controlling parasites on the dog's body are some that can be given internally. Since dosage must be carefully controlled, these preparations should not be used without consulting a veterinarian.

Internal parasites, with the exception of the tapeworm, may be transmitted from a mother dog to the puppies. Infestation may also result from contact with infected bedding or through access to a yard where an infected dog relieves himself. The types that may infest dogs are roundworms, whipworms, tapeworms, hookworms, and heartworms. All cause similar symptoms: a generally unthrifty appearance, stary coat, dull eyes, weakness and emaciation despite a ravenous appetite, coughing, vomiting, diarrhea, and sometimes bloody stools. Not all symptoms are present in every case, of course.

Promiscuous dosing for worms is dangerous and different types of worms require different treatment. So if you suspect your dog has worms, ask your veterinarian to make a microscopic examination of the feces, and to prescribe appropriate treatment if evidence of worm infestation is found.

Clogged anal glands cause intense discomfort, which the dog may attempt to relieve by scooting himself along the floor on his haunches. These glands, located on either side of the anus, secrete a substance that enables the dog to expel the contents of the rectum. If they become clogged, they may give the dog an unpleasant odor and when neglected, serious infection may result. Contents of the glands can be easily expelled into a wad of

cotton, which should be held under the tail with the left hand. Then, using the right hand, pressure should be exerted with the thumb on one side of the anus, the forefinger on the other. The normal secretion is brownish in color, with an unpleasant odor. The presence of blood or pus indicates infection and should be called to the attention of a veterinarian.

Fits, often considered a symptom of worms, may result from a variety of causes, including vitamin deficiencies, or playing to the point of exhaustion. A veterinarian should be consulted when a fit occurs, for it may be a symptom of serious illness.

Distemper takes many and varied forms, so it is sometimes difficult for even experienced veterinarians to diagnose. It is the number one killer of dogs, and although it is not unknown in older dogs, its victims are usually puppies. While some dogs do recover, permanent damage to the brain or nervous system is often sustained. Symptoms may include lethargy, diarrhea, vomiting, reduced appetite, cough, nasal discharge, inflammation of the eyes, and a rise in temperature. If distemper is suspected, a veterinarian must be consulted at once, for early treatment is essential. Effective preventive measures lie in inoculation. Shots for temporary immunity should be given all puppies within a few weeks after whelping, and the permanent inoculations should be given as soon thereafter as possible.

Hardpad has been fairly prevalent in Great Britain for a number of years, and its incidence in the United States is increasing. Symptoms are similar to those of distemper, but as the disease progresses, the pads of the feet harden and eventually peel. Chances of recovery are not favorable unless prompt veterinary care is secured.

Infectious hepatitis in dogs affects the liver, as does the human form, but apparently is not transmissible to man. Symptoms are similar to those of distemper, and the disease rapidly reaches the acute stage. Since hepatitis is often fatal, prompt veterinary treatment is essential. Effective vaccines are available and should be provided all puppies. A combination distemper-hepatitis vaccine is sometimes used.

Leptospirosis is caused by a micro-organism often transmitted by contact with rats, or by ingestion of food contaminated by rats. The disease can be transmitted to man, so anyone caring for an afflicted dog must take steps to avoid infection. Symptoms include vomiting, loss of appetite, diarrhea, fever, depression and lethargy, redness of eyes and gums, and sometimes jaundice. Since permanent kidney damage may result, veterinary treatment should be secured immediately.

Rabies is a disease that is always fatal—and it is transmissible to man. It is caused by a virus that attacks the nervous system and is present in the saliva of an infected animal. When an infected animal bites another, the virus is transmitted to the new victim. It may also enter the body through cuts and scratches that come in contact with saliva containing the virus.

All warm-blooded animals are subject to rabies and it may be transmitted by foxes, skunks, squirrels, horses, and cattle as well as dogs. Anyone bitten by a dog (or other animal) should see his physician immediately, and health and law enforcement officials should be notified. Also, if your dog is bitten by another animal, consult your veterinarian immediately.

In most areas, rabies shots are required by law. Even if not required, all dogs should be given anti-rabies vaccine, for it is an effective preventive measure.

Injuries of a serious nature—deep cuts, broken bones, severe burns, etc.—always require veterinary care. However, the dog may need first aid before being moved to a veterinary hospital.

A dog injured in any way should be approached cautiously, for reactions of a dog in pain are unpredictable and he may bite even a beloved master. A muzzle should always be applied before any attempt is made to move the dog or treat him in any way. The muzzle can be improvised from a strip of cloth, bandage, or even heavy cord, looped firmly around the dog's jaws and tied under the lower jaw. The ends should then be extended back of the neck and tied again so the loop around the jaws will stay in place.

A stretcher for moving a heavy dog can be improvised from a rug or board—preferably two people should be available to transport it. A small dog can be carried by one person simply by grasping the loose skin at the nape of the neck with one hand and placing the other hand under the dog's hips.

Severe bleeding from a leg can be controlled by applying a tourniquet between the wound and the body, but the tourniquet must be loosened at ten-minute intervals. Severe bleeding from head or body can be controlled by placing a cloth or gauze pad over the wound, then applying firm pressure with the hand.

To treat minor cuts, first trim the hair from around the wound, then wash the area with warm soapy water and apply a mild antiseptic such as tincture of metaphen.

Shock is usually the aftermath of severe injury and requires immediate veterinary attention. The dog appears dazed, lips and tongue are pale, and breathing is shallow. The dog should be wrapped in blankets and kept warm, and if possible, kept lying down with his head lower than his body.

Fractures require immediate professional attention. A broken bone should be immobilized while the dog is transported to the veterinarian but no attempt should be made to splint it.

Burns from hot liquid or hot metals should be treated by applying a bland ointment, provided the burned area is small. Burns over large areas should be treated by a veterinarian.

Burns from chemicals should first be treated by flushing the coat with plain water, taking care to protect the dog's eyes and ears. A baking soda solution can then be applied to neutralize the chemical further. If the burned area is small, a bland ointment should be applied. If the burned area is large, more extensive treatment will be required, as well as veterinary care.

Poisoning is more often accidental than deliberate, but which-ever the case, symptoms and treatment are the same. If the poisoning is not discovered immediately, the dog may be found unconscious. His mouth will be slimy, he will tremble, have difficulty breathing, and possibly go into convulsions. Veterinary treatment must be secured immediately.

If you find the dog eating something you know to be poisonous, induce vomiting immediately by repeatedly forcing the dog to swallow a mixture of equal parts of hydrogen peroxide and water. Delay of even a few minutes may result in death. When the con-tents of the stomach have been emptied, force the dog to swallow raw egg white, which will slow absorption of the poison. Then call the veterinarian. Provide him with information as to the type of poison, and follow his advice as to further treatment.

Some chemicals are toxic even though not swallowed, so be-fore using a product, make sure it can be used safely around pets.

Electric shock usually results because an owner negligently leaves an electric cord exposed where the dog can chew on it. If possible, disconnect the cord before touching the dog. Otherwise, yank the cord from the dog's mouth so you will not receive a shock when you try to help him. If the dog is unconscious, arti-ficial respiration and stimulants will be required, so a veterinarian should be consulted at once.

Eye problems of a minor nature—redness or occasional dis-charge—may be treated with a few drops of boric acid solution (2%) or salt solution (1 teaspoonful table salt to 1 pint sterile water). Cuts on the eyeball, bruises close to the eyes, or persistent discharge shoud be treated only by a veterinarian.

Skin problems usually cause persistent itching. However, *fol-licular mange* does not usually do so but is evidenced by moth-eaten-looking patches, especially about the head and along the back. *Sarcoptic mange* produces severe itching and is evidenced by patchy, crusty areas on body, legs, and abdomen. Any evi-dence suggesting either should be called to the attention of a veterinarian. Both require extensive treatment and both may be contracted by humans.

Eczema is characterized by extreme itching, redness of the skin and exudation of serous matter. It may result from a variety of causes, and the exact cause in a particular case may be difficult to determine. Relief may be secured by dusting the dog twice a week with a soothing powder containing a fungicide and an insecticide.

Allergies are not readily distinguished from other skin troubles except through laboratory tests. However, dog owners should be alert to the fact that straw, shavings, or newspapers used for bedding, various coat dressings and shampoos, or simply bathing the dog too often, may produce allergic skin reactions in some dogs. Thus, a change in dog-keeping practices often relieves them.

Symptoms of illness may be so obvious there is no question that the dog is ill, or so subtle that the owner isn't sure whether there is a change from normal or not. *Loss of appetite, malaise* (general lack of interest in what is going on), *and vomiting* may be ignored if they occur singly and persist only for a day. However, in combination with other evidence of illness, such symptoms may be significant and the dog should be watched closely. *Abnormal bowel movements,* especially diarrhea or bloody stools, are cause for immediate concern. *Urinary abnormalities* may indicate infections, and bloody urine is always an indication of a serious condition. When a dog that has long been housebroken suddenly becomes incontinent, a veterinarian should be consulted, for he may be able to suggest treatment or medication that will be helpful.

Persistent coughing is often considered a symptom of worms, but may also indicate heart trouble—especially in older dogs.

Vomiting is another symptom often attributed to worm infestation. Dogs suffering from indigestion sometimes eat grass, apparently to induce vomiting and relieve discomfort.

Stary coat—dull and lackluster—indicates generally poor health and possible worm infestation. *Dull eyes* may result from similar conditions. Certain forms of blindness may also cause the eyes to lose the sparkle of vibrant good health.

Fever is a positive indication of illness and consistent deviation from the normal temperature range of 100 to 102 degrees is cause for concern. To take the dog's temperature, first place the dog on his side. Coat the bulb of a rectal thermometer with petroleum jelly, raise the dog's tail, insert the thermometer to approximately half its length, and hold it in position for two minutes. Clean the thermometer with rubbing alcohol after each use and be sure to shake it down.

A dog that is seriously ill, requiring surgical treatment, transfusions, or intravenous feeding, must be hospitalized. One requiring less complicated treatment is better cared for at home, but it is essential that the dog be kept in a quiet environment. Preferably, his bed should be in a room apart from family activity, yet close at hand, so his condition can be checked frequently. Clean bedding and adequate warmth are essential, as are a constant supply of fresh, cool water, and foods to tempt the appetite.

Special equipment is not ordinarily needed, but the following items will be useful in caring for a sick dog, as well as in giving first aid for injuries:

petroleum jelly	tincture of metaphen
rubbing alcohol	cotton, gauze, and adhesive tape
mineral oil	burn ointment
rectal thermometer	tweezers
hydrogen peroxide	boric acid solution (2%)

If special medication is prescribed, it may be administered in any one of several ways. A pill or small capsule may be concealed in a small piece of meat, which the dog will usually swallow with no problem. A large capsule may be given by holding the dog's mouth open, inserting the capsule as far as possible down the throat, then holding the mouth closed until the dog swallows. Liquid medicine should be measured into a small bottle or test tube. Then, if the corner of the dog's lip is pulled out while the head is tilted upward, the liquid can be poured between the lips and teeth, a small amount at a time. If he refuses to swallow, keeping the dog's head tilted and stroking his throat will usually induce swallowing.

Foods offered the sick dog should be particularly nutritious and easily digested. Meals should be smaller than usual and offered at more frequent intervals. If the dog is reluctant to eat, offer food he particularly likes and warm it slightly to increase aroma and thus make it more tempting.

Housing Your Dog

Every dog should have a bed of his own, snug and warm, where he can retire undisturbed when he wishes to nap. And, especially with a small puppy, it is desirable to have the bed arranged so the dog can be securely confined at times, safe and contented. If the puppy is taught early in life to stay quietly in his box at night, or when the family is out, the habit will carry over into adulthood and will benefit both dog and master.

The dog should never be banished to a damp, cold basement, but should be quartered in an out-of-the-way corner close to the center of family activity. His bed can be an elaborate cushioned affair with electric warming pad, or simply a rectangular wooden box or heavy paper carton, cushioned with a clean cotton rug or towel. Actually, the latter is ideal for a new puppy, for it is snug, easy to clean, and expendable. A "door" can be cut on one side of the box for easy access, but it should be placed in such a way that the dog can still be confined when desirable.

The shipping crates used by professional handlers at dog shows make ideal indoor quarters. They are lightweight but strong, provide adequate air circulation, yet are snug and warm and easily cleaned. For the dog owner who takes his dog along when he travels, a dog crate is ideal, for the dog will willingly stay in his accustomed bed during long automobile trips, and the crate can be taken inside motels or hotels at night, making the dog a far more acceptable guest.

Dog crates are made of chromed metal or wood, and some have tops covered with a special rubber matting so they can be used as grooming tables. Anyone moderately handy with tools can construct a crate similar to the one illustrated on page 35.

Crates come in various sizes, to suit various breeds of dogs. For reasons of economy, the size selected for a puppy should be adequate for use when the dog is full grown. If the area seems too large when the puppy is small, a temporary cardboard partition can be installed to limit the area he occupies.

The dog owner who lives in the suburbs or in the country may want to keep a mature dog outdoors part of the time, in which case an outdoor doghouse should be provided. This type of kennel can also be constructed by the home handyman, but must be more substantial than quarters used indoors.

Outside finish of the doghouse can be of any type, but double wall construction will make for greater warmth in chilly weather. The floor should be smooth and easy to clean, so tongued and grooved boards or plywood are best. To keep the floor from contact with the damp earth, supports should be laid flat on the ground, running lengthwise of the structure. 2 x 4s serve well as supports for doghouses for small or medium breeds, but 4 x 4s should be used for large breeds.

The outdoor kennel must be big enough so that the dog can turn around inside, but small enough so that his body heat will keep it warm in chilly weather. The overall length of the kennel shoud be twice the length of the adult dog, measured from tip of nose to onset of tail. Width of the structure should be approximately three-fourths the length. And height from the floor to the point where the roof begins should be approximately one and a half the adult dog's height at the shoulders. If you build the house when the dog is still a puppy, you can determine his approximate adult size by referring to the Standard for his breed.

An "A" type roof is preferable, and an overhang of six inches all the way around will provide protection from sun and rain. If the roof is hinged to fold back, the interior of the kennel can be cleaned readily.

The entrance should be placed to one side rather than in the center, which will provide further protection against the weather. One of the commercially made door closures of rubber will keep out rain, snow, and wind, yet give the pet complete freedom to enter and leave his home.

The best location for the doghouse is where it will get enough morning sun to keep it dry, yet will not be in full sun during hot afternoons. If possible, the back of the doghouse should be placed toward the prevailing winds.

A fenced run or yard is essential to the outdoor kennel, and the fence must be sturdy enough that the dog cannot break through it, and high enough so he cannot jump or climb over it. The gate should have a latch of a type that can't be opened accidentally. The area enclosed must provide the dog with space to exercise freely, or else the dog must be exercised on the leash every day, for no dog should be confined to a tiny yard day after day without adequate exercise.

The yard must be kept clean and odor free, and the doghouse must be scrubbed and disinfected at frequent intervals. One of the insecticides made especially for use in kennels—one with a four to six weeks' residual effect—should be used regularly on floors and walls, inside and out.

Enough bedding must be provided so the dog can snuggle into it and keep warm in chilly weather. Bedding should either be of a type that is inexpensive, so it can be discarded and replaced frequently, or of a type that can be laundered readily. Dogs are often allergic to fungi found on straw, hay, or grass, and sometimes newspaper ink, but cedar shavings and old cotton rugs and blankets usually serve very well.

The Stone-age Dog

A Spotted Dog from India, "Parent of the Modern Coach dog."

History of
the Genus Canis

The history of man's association with the dog is a fascinating one, extending into the past at least seventy centuries, and involving the entire history of civilized man from the early Stone Age to the present.

The dog, technically a member of the genus *Canis*, belongs to the zoological family group *Canidae,* which also includes such animals as wolves, foxes, jackals, and coyotes. In the past it was generally agreed that the dog resulted from the crossing of various members of the family *Canidae.* Recent findings have amended this theory somewhat, and most authorities now feel the jackal probably has no direct relationship with the dog. Some believe dogs are descended from wolves and foxes, with the wolf the main progenitor. As evidence, they cite the fact that the teeth of the wolf are identical in every detail with those of the dog, whereas the teeth of the jackal are totally different.

Still other authorities insist that the dog always has existed as a separate and distinct animal. This group admits that it is possible for a dog to mate with a fox, coyote, or wolf, but points out that the resulting puppies are unable to breed with each other, although they can breed with stock of the same genus as either parent. Therefore, they insist, it was impossible for a new and distinct genus to have developed from such crossings. They then cite the fact that any dog can be mated with any other dog and the progeny bred among themselves. These researchers point out, too, heritable characteristics that are totally different in the three animals. For instance, the pupil of the dog's eye is round, that of the wolf oblique, and that of the jackal vertical. Tails, too, differ considerably, for tails of foxes, coyotes, and wolves always drop behind them, while those of dogs may be carried over the back or straight up.

Much conjecture centers on two wild dog species that still exist—the Dingo of Australia, and the Dhole in India. Similar in appearance, both are reddish in color, both have rather long, slender jaws, both have rounded ears that stand straight up, and both species hunt in packs. Evidence indicates that they had the same ancestors. Yet, today, they live in areas that are more than 4,000 miles apart.

Despite the fact that it is impossible to determine just when the dog first appeared as a distinct species, archeologists have found definite proof that the dog was the first animal domesticated by man. When man lived by tracking, trapping, and killing game, the dog added to the forces through which man discovered and captured the quarry. Man shared his primitive living quarters with the dog, and the two together devoured the prey. Thus, each helped to sustain the life of the other. The dog assisted man, too, by defending the campsite against marauders. As man gradually became civilized, the dog's usefulness was extended to guarding the other animals man domesticated, and, even before the wheel was invented, the dog served as a beast of burden. In fact, archeological findings show that aboriginal peoples of Switzerland and Ireland used the dog for such purposes long before they learned to till the soil.

Cave drawings from the palaeolithic era, which was the earliest part of the Old World Stone Age, include hunting scenes in which a rough, canine-like form is shown alongside huntsmen. One of these drawings is believed to be 50,000 years old, and gives credence to the theory that all dogs are descended from a primitive type ancestor that was neither fox nor wolf.

Archeological findings show that Europeans of the New Stone Age possessed a breed of dogs of wolf-like appearance, and a similar breed has been traced through the successive Bronze Age and Iron Age. Accurate details are not available, though, as to the external appearance of domesticated dogs prior to historic times (roughly four to five thousand years ago).

Early records in Chaldean and Egyptian tombs show that several distinct and well-established dog types had been developed by about 3700 B.C. Similar records show that the early people of the Nile Valley regarded the dog as a god, often burying it as a mummy in special cemeteries and mourning its death.

Some of the early Egyptian dogs had been given names, such as Akna, Tarn, and Abu, and slender dogs of the Greyhound type and a short-legged Terrier type are depicted in drawings found

Bas-relief of Hunters with Nets and Mastiffs. From the walls of Assurbanipal's palace at Nineveh 668-626 B.C. *British Museum.*

in Egyptian royal tombs that are at least 5,000 years old. The Afghan Hound and the Saluki are shown in drawings of only slightly later times. Another type of ancient Egyptian dog was much heavier and more powerful, with short coat and massive head. These probably hunted by scent, as did still another type of Egyptian dog that had a thick furry coat, a tail curled almost flat over the back, and erect "prick" ears.

Early Romans and Greeks mentioned their dogs often in literature, and both made distinctions between those that hunted by sight and those that hunted by scent. The Romans' canine classifications were similar to those we use now. In addition to dogs comparable to the Greek sight and scent hounds, the ancient Romans had Canes *villatici* (housedogs) and Canes *pastorales* (sheepdogs), corresponding to our present-day working dogs.

The dog is mentioned many times in the Old Testament. The first reference, in Genesis, leads some Biblical scholars to assert that man and dog have been companions from the time man was created. And later Biblical references bring an awareness of the diversity in breeds and types existing thousands of years ago.

As civilization advanced, man found new uses for dogs. Some required great size and strength. Others needed less of these characteristics but greater agility and better sight. Still others needed an accentuated sense of smell. As time went on, men kept those puppies that suited specific purposes especially well and bred them together. Through ensuing generations of selective breeding, desirable characteristics appeared with increasing frequency. Dogs used in a particular region for a special purpose gradually became more like each other, yet less like dogs of other areas used for different purposes. Thus were established the foundations for the various breeds we have today.

The American Kennel Club, the leading dog organization in the United States, divides the various breeds into six "Groups," based on similarity of purposes for which they were developed.

"Sporting Dogs" include the Pointers, Setters, Spaniels, and Retrievers that were developed by sportsmen interested in hunting game birds. Most of the Pointers and Setters are of comparatively recent origin. Their development parallels the development of sporting firearms, and most of them evolved in the British Isles. Exceptions are the Weimaraner, which was developed in Germany, and the Vizsla, or Hungarian Pointer, believed to have been developed by the Magyar hordes that swarmed over Central Europe a thousand years ago. The Irish were among the first to use Spaniels, though the name indicates that the original stock may have come from Spain. Two Sporting breeds, the American Water Spaniel, and the Chesapeake Bay Retriever, were developed entirely in the United States.

"Hounds," among which are Dachshunds, Beagles, Bassets, Harriers, and Foxhounds, are used singly, in pairs, or in packs to "course" (or run) and hunt for rabbits, foxes, and various rodents. But little larger, the Norwegian Elkhound is used in its native country to hunt big game—moose, bear, and deer.

The smaller Hound breeds hunt by scent, while the Irish Wolfhound, Borzoi, Scottish Deerhound, Saluki, and Greyhound hunt by sight. The Whippet, Saluki, and Greyhound are notably fleet of foot, and racing these breeds (particularly the Greyhound) is popular sport.

The Bloodhound is a member of the Hound Group that is known world-wide for its scenting ability. On the other hand, the Basenji is a comparatively rare Hound breed and has the distinction of being the only dog that cannot bark.

"Working Dogs" have the greatest utilitarian value of all modern dogs and contribute to man's welfare in diverse ways. The Boxer, Doberman Pinscher, Rottweiler, German Shepherd, Great Dane, and Giant Schnauzer are often trained to serve as sentries and aid police in patrolling streets. The German Shepherd is especially noted as a guide dog for the blind. The Collie, the various breeds of Sheepdogs, and the two Corgi breeds are known throughout the world for their extraordinary herding ability. And the exploits of the St. Bernard and Newfoundland are legendary, their records for saving lives unsurpassed.

The Siberian Husky and the Alaskan Malamute are noted for tremendous strength and stamina. Had it not been for these hardy Northern breeds, the great polar expeditions might never have taken place, for Admiral Byrd used these dogs to reach points inaccessible by other means. Even today, with our jet-age transportation, the Northern breeds provide a more practical means of travel in frigid areas than do modern machines.

"Terriers" derive their name from the Latin *terra,* meaning

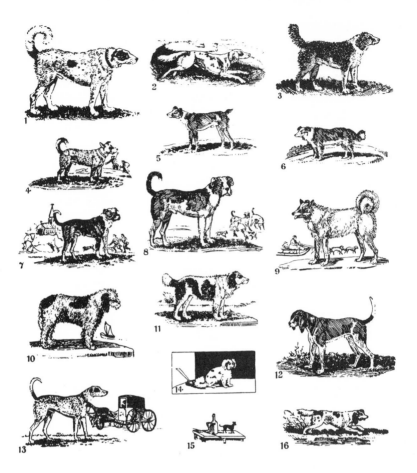

1. The Newfoundland. 2. The English Setter. 3. The Large Water-spaniel. 4. The Terrier. 5. The Cur-dog. 6. The Shepherd's Dog. 7. The Bulldog. 8. The Mastiff. 9. The Greenland Dog. 10. The Rought Water-dog. 11. The Small Water-spaniel. 12. The Old English Hound. 13. The Dalmatian or Coach-dog. 14. The Comporter (very much of a Papillon). 15. "Toy Dog, Bottle, Glass, and Pipe." *From a vignette.* 16. The Springer or Cocker. *From Thomas Bewick's "General History of Quadrupeds" (1790).*

"earth," for all of the breeds in this Group are fond of burrowing. Terriers hunt by digging into the earth to rout rodents and fur-bearing animals such as badgers, woodchucks, and otters. Some breeds are expected merely to force the animals from their dens in order that the hunter can complete the capture. Others are expected to find and destroy the prey, either on the surface or under the ground.

Terriers come in a wide variety of sizes, ranging from such large breeds as the Airedale and Kerry Blue to such small ones as the Skye, the Dandie Dinmont, the West Highland White, and the Scottish Terrier. England, Ireland, and Scotland produced most of the Terrier breeds, although the Miniature Schnauzer was developed in Germany.

"Toys," as the term indicates, are small breeds. Although they make little claim to usefulness other than as ideal housepets, Toy dogs develop as much protective instinct as do larger breeds and serve effectively in warning of the approach of strangers.

Origins of the Toys are varied. The Pekingese was developed as the royal dog of China more than two thousand years before the birth of Christ. The Chihuahua, smallest of the Toys, originated in Mexico and is believed to be a descendant of the Techichi, a dog of great religious significance to the Aztecs, while the Italian Greyhound was popular in the days of ancient Pompeii.

"Non-Sporting Dogs" include a number of popular breeds of varying ancestry. The Standard and Miniature Poodles were developed in France for the purpose of retrieving game from water. The Bulldog originated in Great Britain and was bred for the purpose of "baiting" bulls. The Chowchow apparently originated centuries ago in China, for it is pictured in a bas relief dated to the Han dynasty of about 150 B.C.

The Dalmatian served as a carriage dog in Dalmatia, protecting travelers in bandit-infested regions. The Keeshond, recognized as the national dog of Holland, is believed to have originated in the Arctic or possibly the Sub-Arctic. The Schipperke, sometimes erroneously described as a Dutch dog, originated in the Flemish provinces of Belgium. And the Lhasa Apso came from Tibet, where it is known as "Abso Seng Kye," the "Bark Lion Sentinel Dog."

During the thousands of years that man and dog have been closely associated, a strong affinity has been built up between the two. The dog has more than earned his way as a helper, and his faithful, selfless devotion to man is legendary. The ways in which the dog has proved his intelligence, his courage, and his dependability in situations of stress are amply recorded in the countless tales of canine heroism that highlight the pages of history, both past and present.

Dogs in Woodcuts. (*1st row*) (LEFT) "Maltese dog with shorter hair";
(RIGHT) "Spotted sporting dog trained to catch game"; (*2nd row*) (LEFT)
Sporting white dog; (RIGHT) "Spanish dog with floppy ears": (*3rd row*)
(LEFT) "French dog"; (RIGHT) "Mad dog of Grevinus"; (*4th row*) (LEFT)
Hairy Maltese dog; (RIGHT) "English fighting dog . . . of horrid aspect." *From
Aldrovandus (1637).*

History of the Beagle

It is virtually impossible to determine an exact date for the establishment of the Beagle as a separate breed. It cannot even be determined that the modern Beagle is the sole product of England. Breeds that have been created in the last one hundred to two hundred years are relatively easy to trace because of the conscientious record keeping on the part of the breeders. Such is not the case, however, with the ancient breeds that have gone through centuries of evolution to bring into being the purebred dogs that exist today.

This is true of the Beagle. The breed, or to be more precise, the type has existed for centuries. The early existence of the Beagle-type dog is evidenced in both literature and art, which have frequently served to establish historical authenticity when written proof is lacking.

Small domesticated hunting dogs appeared centuries before the birth of Christ in the lands at the eastern end of the Mediterranean. This is testified to by the early Greek writings of Xenophon in the fourth century B.C. In *Cynegeticus,* a treatise on the hunting of hare, wild boar, and deer, he refers to the small hunting dogs of the period. These dogs hunted in packs and were Scent Dogs that seemed to be endowed with singing or yodeling qualities similar to those of the present-day Beagle.

References to these small Hounds were frequent in both Greek and Roman literature for several centuries. The Romans divided dogs into six different categories according to their value to man: Fighting Dogs *(Pugnaces),* Scent Dogs *(Nares Sagaces),* Coursing Sight Dogs *(Pedibus Celeres),* Hunting Dogs *(Venatici),* Herding Dogs *(Pastorales),* and House Dogs *(Villatici).* The early ancestors of the Beagle would have come from the Scent Dogs.

These Scent Hounds were probably carried north across Europe by traveling huntsmen. The small dogs were used on small game, allowing their larger cousins to pursue such large animals as wild boar, deer, and bear. That these dogs should be brought to England seems only natural for the island abounded with small game, especially rabbits. There are frequent references to such small Scent Hounds dating from the thirteenth century. References are almost never made to a single dog, but rather to the packs in which they were hunted.

In 1413, Edward, the Second Duke of York, wrote *The Master of the Game,* which, by the way, was also the official title for the position he held in the royal household. In discussing his duties, he made frequent reference to the small Scent Hounds of the court.

The Book of St. Albans, written in 1486 by Juliana Berners, the Prioress of Sopwell, speaks of the thirteen different breeds of dogs that were then popular. Two of these, the Kennet and the Rache, have frequently been cited as early examples of the modern day Beagle. It would seem that the Rache was more closely related to the Foxhound because of its size. The Kennet, being the smaller of the two breeds, would be a more likely ancestor for the Beagle.

The word Beagle began to appear in British literature toward the end of the fifteenth century. The first such reference to *begle* cited by the *Oxford English Dictionary* is from *Squire lowe Degre* dating from c. 1475. From that time on the Beagle maintained its own identity and name. The origins of the word Beagle are somewhat unclear. Some evidence has been advanced that the present name is a corruption of the medieval French word *Bégueule,* which was formed from *béer,* meaning *to open wide,* and *gueule,* for *throat.* The name would then refer to the Beagle's singing while on the trail rather than to his scenting abilities. Considering that the early ancestors undoubtedly passed through France on their way to England, it is quite possible that such a name was brought with them and later corrupted by non-French speaking peasants in England. Some doubts can also be cast on such an origin when it is remembered that the present-day work in French for this dog is the English word Beagle.

Sixteenth century British law forbade poaching on the lands belonging to the crown. This represented large sections of the country and undoubtedly worked great hardships on the lower classes of the day. Some slight exceptions were made, however, from time to time. One of these exceptions was made for the Beagle.

The king was basically interested in the hunting of large game, especially the stag. While he occasionally would hunt rabbits, it was certainly not his favorite sport. Considering the prolificness of the rabbit, it is easy to understand why some relaxing of controls would be needed to keep the rabbit population down. Allowing

A nineteenth century etching of the English Beagles Ch. Ringwood and Little Un.

Beagle-type dogs in to hunt on occasion would serve as this necessary control.

The Beagle was considered essentially a rabbit dog. He was hunted in packs and controlled by the Master of the Hounds, who used a hunting horn. Beagles were hunted both from horseback and on foot. They frequently proved too fast to be followed on foot, and when their trail led through the underbrush, hunting from horseback proved impossible. It was just such conditions that led to the development of such other breeds as the Basset Hound, which had strength and stamina but did not have the speed of the Beagle.

References are regularly made to the Pocket Beagles of Queen Elizabeth I (1533-1603). These were really miniatures of today's much larger Beagles. The Pocket Beagles were between eight and twelve inches, and were considered more valuable when they were of the smaller measurement. While others of the period used the Pocket Beagles for the hunt, the Queen did not. She treated them as lap dogs and considered them house pets, much in the fashion of the Toy dogs.

A nineteenth century etching of the English Beagles Giant and Ringlet.

Head study of Ch. Ravenswood Softwalker, owned by Mr. and Mrs. Donald Barnes.

Head study of Ch. Kinsman Prim II, owned by Lee S. Wade.

Four famous Kinsman champions, all bred by Lee S. Wade and shown throughout the United States and Canada. Left to right: Ch. Kinsman Little Merryman, great grandsire; International Ch. Kinsman Jimmy Valentine, son; International Ch. Travis Court Terwilliger, grandsire; and International Ch. Kinsman High Jinks, sire.

Succeeding rulers of England, notably William of Orange (1689-1702) and King George IV (1762-1830), were avid hunters and regularly rode over a pack of Beagles. In the nineteenth century, Prince Albert, the consort of Queen Victoria, was especially proud of his pack of all white Beagles. He was a strong advocate of the hunt and devoted much time to his special dogs.

Throughout the eighteenth and nineteenth centuries, riding to the Hounds was an extremely popular sport among the landed gentry. The Beagle and the Foxhound were well established as breeds even though they differed somewhat in size and conformation from the present-day specimens.

As popularity increased toward the end of the nineteenth century, a need for some type of organization and standardization was felt. This led to the founding of The Beagle Club in 1890. This was followed one year later by the establishment of the Association of Masters of Harriers and Beagles. Both of these clubs sought to improve the breed and to standardize breeding programs. A secondary benefit to breeders was the initiation of an official record-keeping organization. Since a certain portion of the pleasure in the sport comes from the records dogs establish, having an official and impartial office for the preservation of records was an added advantage.

While the English Kennel Club was not established until 1873, a group of interested breeders had more or less formalized classification of dogs as early as 1859. Dogs were divided into two categories: Sporting and Non-Sporting. This division was formalized in 1881 and continued until 1947 when Sporting was further subdivided into Hounds, Gundogs, and Terriers. The present Group divisions in England are similar to those in the United States. They are: Hound, Gundogs, Working, Terrier, Toys, and Utility. While these divisions may correspond between the two countries, the same dogs are not necessarily in the same Groups in both countries. The Shih Tzu, for instance, is in the Utility Group instead of the Toy Group, and the Schnauzers are also in the Utility Group instead of in the Terrier and Working Groups.

For many years there were two varieties of Beagles in England. One variety consisted of dogs under ten inches at the withers and the other of dogs between ten inches and sixteen inches. The miniature size was referred to as the Pocket Beagle. Popularity of the Pocket Beagle continued until shortly before World War II, when the under ten inch classes were dropped because breeders

Ch. Elsy's Trailblazer, owned by Roy and Rita Randel.

Ch. Silver Star Whata Guy, owned by Billie R. Huggins.

Ch. Johjean Joker of Do-Mor, owned by William and Cecile Busch.

were having difficulty in maintaining the same qualities in miniature. Some interest has occasionally been expressed in recent years to reestablish this division, but at present there is still only discussion.

During the eighteenth and nineteenth centuries there was great variation in coat texture. This was the result of outcrossing with other breeds to bring in certain characteristics which the Beagle seemed to lack. For a period of time in some sections of England the Beagle was crossed with some of the Terriers in the hope of making him a more fierce hunter. Being bred to the taller, more leggy Terriers would not do much to the size of the Beagle, considering the fact that there was already a considerable spread in size. It did, however, have a great effect on his coat. There are frequent references for a considerable period of time to the wirehaired Beagle, or to the Beagle with the rough coat. It is hard to imagine such a Beagle today, but for some time such a specimen was a canine reality. The formalization of a Standard for the breed did eliminate this quality that could easily have produced still another variety of the Beagle.

In 1912 Mr. F. Claude Kempson published *The Trinity Foot Beagles*. The subtitle for this work is "An informal record of Cambridge sport and sportsmen during the past fifty years." Mr. Kempson was very familiar with hunting practices of the day and chronicled with great authority the development of hunting packs by the nobility during the last half of the nineteenth century.

Prior to the 1870s, most Beagles in the United States were of the short-legged variety and had much more white on their bodies than do present-day dogs. About this time General Rowett of Carlinville, Illinois, began to import some specimens from England. Two such Beagles were Rosey and Dolly, who served as foundation stock for his long-lived kennel. With Rowett's death the stock of this kennel was acquired by Pottinger Dorsey and C. Staley Doub of Maryland, who carried on with his breeding program.

Other early importers were Norman Elmore Grouby of Connecticut, who imported Ringwood, and C. H. Turner, who imported Sam and Warrior. Other nineteenth century importers were: James L. Kernochan, the Reverend Philip Honeywood, and a Mr. Arnold of Rhode Island.

The National Beagle Club was founded in 1888 and began holding regular trials after that date. The Beagle club was a natural development of the interest generated by the formulation of the Standard that was written in 1887.

Ch. The Balladier of Starcrest, owned by Robert and Louise Merrill.

Ch. Elsy's Gay Lass of Ollieanne, owned by W. S. Elsy.

Ch. Confer's Cindy Too, owned by Patricia E. Confer.

Bench Beagle Kennels

Beagles have always been among the most popular breeds in the United States. During the 1940s and early 1950s they ranked second, after the Cocker Spaniel. During the late 1950s they were the most popular of all dogs, with annual registrations that reached almost 70,000. During the 1960s, when registrations dropped to the low 60,000s, they slipped to fourth in popularity, after the Poodle, the German Shepherd, and the Dachshund. They are currently ranked third, having passed the Dachshund. The Poodle still retains its popularity and its first-place rank after more than a dozen years. This is very significant when it is remembered that the annual registration of dogs is well over one million.

There are many kennels that breed and show Beagles today, and still others that were once prominent but are no longer operating. The bench show kennels that have been selected to be included in this chapter are those that have been most active in the last ten to fifteen year period. The listing of these kennels is in alphabetical order according to kennel prefix.

Alpha-Centauri Kennel, located in Mason, Illinois, is owned by professional handler Robert Goodfellow and his wife, Judy. The winners from this kennel include: Ch. Alpha-Centauri Geisha Girl, Ch. Alpha-Centauri Drummer Boy, and Ch. Alpha-Centauri Sam Junior.

The Brandenburg Kennel of John Herrington is located in Brandenburg, Kentucky. Winners carrying this kennel title include: Ch. Hit Parade of Brandenburg, Ch. Lazy Bones of Brandenburg, and Ch. Bennet of Brandenburg.

Garland B. Moore is the owner of Buglair Kennel located in Atwater, California. Many fine Beagles carry this prefix. Ch. Buglair Topper was a Specialty Best-in-Show winner while Ch. Buglair Tex is the winner of a Group First. Other title holders from this kennel include: Ch. Buglair Top of the Mark, Ch. Buglair Top Copy, and Ch. Buglair Politician of Hark Ye.

Professional handler William Busch and his wife, Cecile, established their kennel in Cape Girardeau, Missouri, in 1959. Their foundation stud was Ch. Clark's Lackawana Tony, the last cham-

Ch. Busch's Bonnie Prince Charlie (left), winning the Stud Dog Class at the 1972 National Beagle Specialty, with Ch. Busch's Nuts to You of Brendons and Ch. Twinkletoes Merry Busch Imp.

Ch. Busch's Gin Rickey, owned by William and Cecile Busch.

Ch. Pine Bend's Harvey Wallbanger, owned by the Leslie Scholles.

pion from Ch. Thornridge Wrinkles, the breed's all-time top producing stud. Ch. Johjean Joker of Do Mor joined the kennel in 1966. Since that time he has sired more than thirty champions.

Ch. Busch's Bonnie Prince Charlie, a Joker son and the sire of numerous champions, won the Stud Dog Class at the National Specialty in 1972. His son Ch. Busch's Nuts to You of Brendons is a multiple Best-in-Show and Specialty winner. One of his sons, Ch. Busch's Gin Rickey, won his first Group First his first time out at seven months of age. Rickey was the top winning fifteen inch Beagle in the United States in both 1974 and 1975.

Busch's Little Dixie is the dam of ten champions, five of these from a single litter sired by Joker. Ch. Busch's Sweet As Candy is also the dam of ten champions while Ch. Busch's Dixie Duplicator is the dam of seven champions. They are both Little Dixie daughters.

Ch. Busch's Hansom Ransom was exported to Japan, where he sired a Best-in-Show winner. Ch. Busch's Disc Jockey and Ch. Busch's Fancy Free were exported to Dr. Arie Preschel in Venezuela, where they have since completed Venezuelan championships—with both having earned Group Firsts.

Colegren Kennel is owned by Virginia Coleman and is located in Durham, North Carolina. Some title holders carrying this kennel prefix are Ch. Colegren Applause, C.D., Ch. Colegren Motor Mouse, Ch. Colegren Check Mate, and Ch. Colegren Duke Devil.

Patricia E. Confer has her kennel in Springfield, Missouri. With a very limited breeding program Miss Confer has produced three Group-Winning bitches: Ch. Confer's Super Sandy, her daughter Ch. Confer's Hecate, and Ch. Confer's Cindy Too. Other winners include Ch. Confer's Ellen Grae, Ch. Confer's Midget of Vanowen, and Ch. Confer's Knight of Vanowen.

Double-Jac Kennel of San Antonio, Texas, is owned by Mr. and Mrs. Jack Potts. Their winners include Ch. Double-Jac Matches, Ch. Double-Jac Texas Taxes, and Ch. Double-Jac Sundance Gal, owned by Mr. and Mrs. Robert McLean.

Mrs. Clark Draper's kennel is located in Richmond, Virginia. Among the winners carrying the Draper prefix are Ch. Draper's Lemon Drop Kid, Ch. Draper's Lemon Drop Lil Abner, and Ch. Draper's Lemon Drop Pixie. Ch. Draper's Lemon Drop Daisy Mae is a Group winner and is owned by John and Patricia White. Ch. Draper's Rusty Rebel, C.D.X., is owned by Wendy J. Joy.

W. Stanley and Mariette D. Elsy have raised Beagles for more

Ch. Confer's Ellen Grae,
owned by Marcia Carlyle.

Ch. Junior's Powerplay,
C.D., owned by Dick
Johnson.

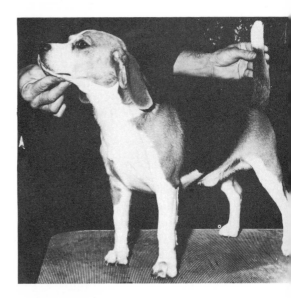

Ch. Windyroc's Dandy
Dude, owned by the
Thomas Schmidts.

than fifty years. Their Elsy Kennel, located in Portland, Oregon, has been the starting point for many Beagle kennels throughout the years. Winners include Ch. Elsy's Show Boat, Ch. Elsy's Block Buster, and Ch. Elsy's Rumboat. Double title holders include Ch. Elsy's Montague, C.D., Ch. Elsy's Storm Trooper, C.D., Ch. Elsy's Trick or Treat, C.D., and Ch. Elsy's Portland Punch, C.D. Ch. Elsy's Diamond Jerry, a Group winner, was exported to Mrs. Thelma Gray in England, where he established a remarkable record both as a show dog and as a top producing stud. He won a Group First at his first show in England, won a C.C. at Crufts, and was Best in Show at the National Beagle Specialty. For five years he was also the winner of the Stud Dog Class at the Specialty—one year having twenty-five of his get entered at that show.

The Foyscroft Kennel of Tom and Marcia Foy is located in Attleboro, Massachusetts. This kennel is represented mainly with fifteen inch winners such as Ch. Foyscroft Highland Corky, Ch. Foyscroft Triple Crown, Ch. Foyscroft Davey Crockett, and Ch. Foyscroft Triple Bonzai, owned by Elizabeth Wasserman.

Fulmont Beagles is operated by William and Julie Fulkerson in Lenoir City, Tennessee. Among their winners are Ch. Fulmont's Fable, Ch. Fulmont's Flower Child, and Ch. Fulmont's Megen.

The Gaycroft Kennel of William and Marion Hans is located in Scranton, Pennsylvania. Winning bitches from this kennel are Ch. Gaycroft Carol, Ch. Gaycroft Cricket, Ch. Gaycroft Crystal, and Ch. Gaycroft Claudia.

Winners from the Heard's Kennel in Twin Falls, Idaho, include Ch. Heard's Patsy Ann, Ch. Heard's Henry, Ch. Heard's November, and Ch. Heard's Hercules.

James and Althea Harvey have their Jana Kennel in California. Among the winners are Ch. Jana Will O-Whisp, Ch. Jana Raider, Ch. Jana Tommy Hawk, and Ch. Jana Zipper.

Jaycee's Kennel of Bill Green is located in the Southwest. Champions include Ch. Jaycee's Sugar and Spice, Ch. Jaycee's Copper Penny, and Ch. Jaycee's Mystic Charm. The Group-First winning Ch. Jaycee's Bugle Billie of Saxen-D is owned by nine-year-old David B. Saxen.

John and Jean Refieuna established their Johjean Kennel in La Grange, Illinois. Dozens of champions carry this kennel prefix and many other winners sired by Johjean dogs owe credit to this kennel. Best-in-Show Specialty winners include Ch. Johjean Pop Corn and Ch. Johjean Jubilation T. Cornbal. Other winners are Ch. Johjean Jenner Jacket, C.D., Ch. Johjean Jabal, Ch. Johjean Jinger Drop, and Ch. Johjean Jentle John Janzoom.

Junior's Beagles are owned by Dick Johnson of Miami, Florida. He has been represented by Ch. Junior's Belle Star, C.D.X., Ch. Junior's Powerplay, C.D., Ch. Junior's Sonny Boy, and Ch. Junior's Windy Whim, C.D.

Kings Creek Kennel was originally owned by Howard Lagerquist but later sold to the Venable Leathers of Georgia. Winners with this prefix are Ch. Kings Creek Satan's Doll, Ch. Kings Creek Major Wilson, Ch. Kings Creek Stagerlee, and Ch. Kings Creek Quarterback.

Lee S. Wade's Kinsman Kennel is now located in South El Monte, California. Ch. Kinsman High Jinks is a top producing sire with more than forty champion get. Ch. Kinsman Little Dickens is the sire of ten champions, as is Ch. Kinsman Little Merryman.

Lawndale's Kennel is owned by professional handler Herb Hardt of Belleville, Illinois. Winners with this prefix are Ch. Lawndale's Miss Impossible, Ch. Lawndale's Hallmark, and Ch. Lawndale's Trademark. The Group winning bitch Ch. Lawndale's Dancing Doll is owned by John and Norma Struwe of Springfield, Illinois.

Meado Glo Kennel, located in the Midwest, is the property of Mrs. Elsie Jackson. Among the fifteen inch winners are Ch. Meado Glo Archer, Ch. Meado Glo Northern Star, Ch. Meado Glo Gold Coin, and Ch. Meado Glo Painted Windbell, owned by Howard Meier.

The Page Mill Kennel of California has established an enviable record in the show ring. Some of the champions are Ch. Page Mill Copy Mark, Ch. Page Mill Trademark, and Ch. Page Mill Wind Drift. Special attention is called to Ch. Page Mill Landmark, who is also a Tracking Dog.

Perky's Kennel is located in Livonia, Michigan, and is owned by Herman J. Pyrkosz. Winners here include Ch. Perky's Shadrack Dandy, Ch. Perky's Ring Master, Ch. Perky's Ruff N'Ready Rusty, and Ch. Perky's Binka.

Mr. and Mrs. Leslie Scholle established their Pine Bend Kennel in Shorewood, Minnesota. Their foundation bitch, Ch. Alpha-Centauri's Miss Fancy, produced Ch. Pine Bend's Harvey Wallbanger, who went Best in Show his first time out at seven months at the Wisconsin Beagle Club Specialty in 1973.

Ralph Alderfer of Souderton, Pennsylvania, is the owner of Pin Oaks Kennel. He is represented by Ch. Pin Oaks Mister Roberts, Ch. Pin Oaks Gallant Gay Lad, and Ch. Pin Oaks Charming Don

Juan. Ch. Pin Oaks Lil Abner is owned by Leona and Scott Ryan, and Ch. Pin Oaks Royal Delight is owned by April Randall.

Pixshire's Kennel is owned by Mrs. Virginia Flowers. The foundation stud was Ch. Wright-Eager Texas Tripper and the foundation bitch was Ch. Busch's Sweet As Candy. Winners include Ch. Pixshire's Texas Quarterback, Ch. Pixshire's Texas Tracker, Ch. Pixshire's Millionaire, and Ch. Pixshire's High Opinion. Ch. Navan Triple Trouble Rick, a Specialty and all breed Best-in-Show winner, is co-owned by Virginia Flowers and Nancy Vanstrum.

Ravenwood Kennel was established by Donald and Margaret Barnes in Brighton, Colorado, in 1959. Some of their winners are Ch. Ravenwood Passing Fancy, Ch. Ravenwood Softwalker, Ch. Ravenwood Touch of Midas, and Ch. Ravenwood Hamlin Harmony.

The Ridgeland Kennel of Harlan C. Cannon was established in Colfax, Iowa, in 1958. An early interest in field Beagles was finally extended to bench dogs. Winners include Ch. Ridgeland's Jasper, Ch. Ridgeland's Chardon Gabriel, Ch. Ridgeland's Bugle Boy, and Ch. Ridgeland's Tuff Guy, who is co-owned by Damaris Wright.

Mary Shuart of Miami, Florida, established her kennel under the Robin's prefix, but has since changed it to Teloca Beagles. Winners are Ch. Robin's A Boy Named Sue, Ch. Robin's Joyous Noel, Ch. Robin's Here Comes Charlie, and Ch. Robin's LUV.

Nunzio Rubino's kennel is located in Lambertville, New Jersey. Champions are Ch. Rubino's Skip, Ch. Rubino's Go Go, Ch. Rubino's Turvy, and Ch. Rubino's Traveling Man.

Robert and Louise Merrill established their Starcrest Kennel in Los Gatos, California. Winners here are represented by Ch. Trick or Treat of Starcrest. American and Canadian Ch. Gremlin's Imp of Starcrest is a Specialty B.O.V. winner from the classes.

Sunnymeade Kennel is owned by Bob Henry of Indiana. His winners include Ch. Sunnymeade Rosebud, Ch. Sunnymead Captain Gun, Ch. Sunnymeade Judge, and Ch. Sunnymeade Little Doll—a multiple Group-First winner and the dam of ten champions.

Thornridge Kennel is represented by the all-time top sire of bench champions in the breed, Ch. Thornridge Wrinkles, who sired seventy-six bench champions. Ch. Thornridge Toney, Wrinkle's grandsire, was the sire of thirty-four champions. Other winners are Ch. Thornridge Comet, Ch. Thornridge Showman, Ch. Thornridge Ebony, Ch. Thornridge Jenny, and Ch. Thornridge Prim.

Ch. Jaycee's Bugle Billy of Saxen-D, owned by David Saxen.

Multiple Best-in-Show and Specialty winner Ch. Rock A Plenty's Wild Oats, owned by Tom and Marcia Foy.

Ch. The Whim's Come-uppance, owned by Mrs. A. C. Musladin.

Timeric's Kennel is located in Effingham, Illinois, and is owned by Mr. and Mrs. Fred Hicks. Winners are Ch. Timeric's Dashing Dandy, Ch. Timeric's Tiddleywink, Ch. Timeric's Jonah, and Ch. Timeric's Molly, C.D.

Travis Court Kennel is represented by a number of top producing studs, including Ch. Travis Court Terwilliger, with seven; his son Ch. Travis Court General Justice, with sixteen; and his son Ch. Travis Court Sugar Foot, with five champions.

Two sisters, Mrs. Mildred Loew of New York and Mrs. Valentine Davies of California, own Validay Kennel. Among the more than forty champions are Ch. Validay Cinderella, Ch. Validay Star Stream, Ch. Validay Bravo, and Ch. Validay Jove.

Evelyn Droge of Keswick, Virginia, owns Wagon Wheels Kennel. Among the more than thirty champions are Ch. Wagon Wheels Windjammer, Ch. Wagon Wheels Storm Cloud, C.D., Ch. Wagon Wheels Doctor, C.D., and Ch. Wagon Wheels Love, C.D.

Wal-Dor's Kennel is located in Canada. Carrying the kennel prefix was the great Best-in-Show winner, Ch. Wal-Dor's Skipper, owned by J. W. Blankenbakers. Other champions are Ch. Wal-Dor's Bonnie, Ch. Wal-Dor's Princess, and Ch. Wal-Dor's Flying Dutchman, C.D.

Dr. and Mrs. A. C. Musladin have their The Whim's Kennel in Los Gatos, California. Top winners carrying the prefix are Ch. The Whim's Touch-Me-Not, the top winning thirteen inch Beagle in 1975, Ch. The Whim's Cock of the Walk, Ch. The Whim's Chatterbox, Ch. The Whim's Buckeye, and Ch. The Whim's Hucklebuck, owned by David and Linda Hiltz.

Margaret White of Puyallup, Washington, owns White Acres Kennel. Dogs from this kennel are Ch. White Acres Sirius, Ch. White Acres Jim Dandy, Ch. White Acres Tradition, and Ch. White Acres Page Boy, owned by Carl and Minerva Harris.

Jan Schmidt of Bartlesville, Oklahoma, owns Windyroc's Kennel. Typey winners from this kennel are Ch. Windyroc's Angel, Ch. Windyroc's Creme Puff, Ch. Windyroc's Dandy Dude, and Ch. Windyroc's Buster.

Charles and Jeannette Wright of Jefferson City, Missouri, are owners of Wright-Eager Kennel. The Wrights are helped both in the kennel and in the show ring by all of their children. Beagles here are a family joy. Among the more than forty winners are Ch. Wright-Eager Hardy Boy, Ch. Wright-Eager Ruffled Feathers, Ch. Wright-Eager Gay Knight, and Ch. Wright-Eager Texas Tripper.

Field Ch. Pearson Creek
Barbara, owned by the George
Nixons.

Futurity and Derby Field Ch. Pearson Creek Carson, owned by the George Nixons.

Field Ch. Pearson Creek
Countess, owned by the George
Nixons.

Field Trial Kennels

Raising and training field Beagles has been an extremely popular sport in the United States for more than one hundred years. Formalizing such training and establishing competitive trials for these dogs is, however, a more recent development. The National Beagle Club was established in 1888 and held its first field trials in the same year. These first trials were divided for thirteen inch and fifteen inch entries. There were special classes for derbies and four classes for packs. Kansas jack rabbits were used in these trials, which was an improvement over the smaller German hares used elsewhere.

Field trial Beagles have been bred by many individuals and many kennels since the establishment of the club. Many kennels were active only for a brief period of time because their winning depended on one outstanding dog that was not able to reproduce his own quality. Other kennels were dedicated more to breeding than to the actual trials themselves, allowing others to carry forward their kennel title.

Packs were established on the East Coast and in the Midwest in the second half of the nineteenth century. These packs served as foundation stock for many of the present-day kennels.

It is evident from a study of the total number of field trial champions and the total number of Beagles registered, that only a very small percentage of Beagles ever attains the title of field trial champion. The numbers for a recent five-year period range from a low of three-tenths of one percent to a high of seven-tenths of one percent for a particular year. It is, therefore, to the credit of the breeder and trainer that a Beagle ever attains the coveted title.

Since it would be impossible to discuss all winning dogs and kennels, some limitations had to be established. The following alphabetical listing has been limited to those kennels that have been active in the past quarter century.

Beechline Beagles is owned by Bob Beech and is located in Stokesdale, North Carolina. Dogs at this kennel receive extensive training in a sixty-five acre enclosure. Winning stud dogs at Beechline are Field Ch. Pearson Creek Mickey, Field Ch. Villa Ridge Limbo, and Field Ch. Houston's Bonne. Mickey is a line-

Ch. Alpha-Centauri's
Fancy Miss, owned by the
Leslie Scholles.

Int. Ch. Busch's Fancy
Free, owned by Dr. Arie
Preschel of Venezuela.

Ch. Ridgeland Chardon
Gabriel, owned by Harlan
Cannon.

bred dog with heavy crosses to Field Ch. Pearson Creek Stub. Limbo and Bonne are line bred to Field Ch. Wind Creek Limbo.

Black Walnut Beagles, located in New Park, Pennsylvania, is owned by Hugh Lloyd. A young winner is Derby Field Ch. Black Walnut Limbo, already the sire of a champion. Other winning studs here are Field Ch. Tate Cove Bobby and Field Ch. Tate Cove Bonanza.

Cambridge, Maryland, is the site of Philip McGrath's Boundry Line Kennel. Three half-brothers sired by Field Ch. Contentnea Bag Pipe are: Field Ch. Boundry Line Bag Pipe, Derby Field Ch. Boundry Line Sand Bag, and Derby Field Ch. Boundry Line Bag Boy. That the dams are of three different lines testifies to the quality of the sire.

Larry Adams established his Bun-E-Line Beagles in Dora, Alabama. Field Ch. Bun-E-Line Bondsman has sired nearly fifty field champions and is the sire of the great Wind Creek Limbo, who in turn has produced just under one hundred field champions. Other young winners at this kennel are Field Ch. Humtown Shadrack and Field Ch. Dickie's Syndicate.

Neil Clark located his kennel in North Java, New York. His line is based on his winning stud, Field Ch. Pearson Creek Moe, who has sired more than three dozen champions with many others well on their way to the title. Field Ch. Hawkeye Moe, a young son, seems to be destined to follow in his sire's paw prints.

Cobby's Kennel is owned by Willard Cobb and located in Graham, North Carolina. Field Ch. Cobby's Piper has sired more than a dozen winners so far. Two of his winning get are Field Ch. Cobby's Friday and Field Ch. Whittemore Sam.

Robert Connell of Boothwyn, Pennsylvania, leads his stud force with Field Ch. Connell's Checkmate. Among Checkmate's winning get are Field Ch. Connell's Conversation, Field Ch. Connell's Goldie, and Field Ch. Connell's Millie.

Contentnea Beagles is located in Snow Hill, North Carolina. Two thirteen inch dogs establishing records as winners and sires are Derby Field Ch. Contentnea Bag Pipe and Field Ch. V-Line Joe.

Dickie's Kennel is owned by Fred Dickie of Wampum, Pennsylvania. A third generation winner from this kennel is Field Ch. Dickie's Art, who is the son of Field Ch. Dickie's Nancy II and the grandson of Field Ch. Dickie's Syndicate. Art has already sired a half dozen champions.

Hartford, Connecticut, is the home of Falconridge Beagles, which is owned by William D. Shew. Field Ch. Falconridge Goldfinger is the result of a full-brother, full-sister breeding. This brother and sister, both champions, were from a litter in which seven attained their titles. One of Goldfinger's winning sons is Field Ch. Falconridge Little Joe.

Gates City Beagles, located in Summerfield, North Carolina, is owned by C. M. Jordan. The stud, Derby Field Ch. Waltman's Joe, who produced twenty-six winners, is the son of Field Ch. Joe's Nixon, sire of forty-one winners. Waltman's Joe is the sire of Derby Field Ch. Gate City Bill. Field Ch. Loudermilk's M. Dean is another young stud in this kennel.

Hurricane, West Virginia, is the home of John Gatens' Hillbilly Beagles. Field Ch. Redneb Percy, the sire of more than a dozen champions, is the son of the all-time great sire, Ch. Pearson Creek Carson.

Pat Izzi operates a small kennel in Cranston, Rhode Island. Already the sire of a couple of champions is Field Ch. Pearson Creek Casey, who is line bred on the great Field Ch. Pearson Creek Stub.

Kidd's Kennel of J. W. Kidd is located in Huntersville, North Carolina. Field Ch. Sacajawea Steady Eddie, a Carson son, is the sire of fourteen champions. Another stud dog in this kennel is Field Ch. Kidd's Stub.

King's Kennel of David L. King is in Caldwell, Ohio. The stud force of this kennel is based on two litter mates: Field Ch. Pearson Creek Danny and Field Ch. Pearson Creek Fred. Danny is the sire of twenty-one champions, while Fred is the sire of twenty-two.

General Myrick established his kennel in Warrior, Alabama. Three winners carrying the kennel banner are Field Ch. Myrick's Michael, Field Ch. Myrick's Mule, and Field Ch. Myrick's Chester. Mule and Michael are full brothers and are by Field Ch. Pearson Creek Danny. Winning bitches from this kennel include Field Ch. Myrick's Mag, the dam of Mule and Michael, and Field Ch. Myrick's Big Maude, their granddam.

Bob Oliver and Dan Bell use as a stud dog for their kennel in New Jersey Field Ch. Pearson Creek Farmer, a thirteen inch dog who has already sired more than a half dozen field champions.

Akron, Ohio, is the location of Ben Patrick's kennel. His stud force includes Field Ch. Meddlesome Needler, a Wind Creek Limbo son, and Field Ch. Meddlesome Ned, a Needler son.

Pearson Creek Beagles is the all-time top producing kennel of the field trial Beagle. The kennel is located in Springfield, Missouri, and is owned by Mr. and Mrs. George Nixon. In less than a ten-year period, thirteen Pearson Creek studs have produced almost five hundred field trial champions. Twelve of these dogs are still producing and many of them are very young dogs.

The great Field Ch. Pearson Creek Stub produced seventy-six field champions, although he was not used at stud after he was two and a half years old. Stub was the result of a half-brother, half-sister breeding. Stub was bred to his litter sister, Field Ch. Pearson Creek Barbara, a dam of five champions, and produced Field Ch. Pearson Creek Carson, who is the only Derby and Futurity winner in the breed. Carson is the sire of one hundred sixteen field champions and that number could eventually double.

Other leading studs at the home kennel are Field Ch. Pearson Creek Barbarian, with forty-eight champions; Field Ch. Pearson Creek Banjo, with nineteen; Field Ch. Pearson Creek Nick, with nineteen; and Field Ch. Pearson Creek Casanova with thirteen. Pearson Creek winners in other kennels include: Field Ch. Pearson Creek Piper, with thirty-nine champions; Field Ch. Pearson Creek Moe, with thirty-three; Field Ch. Pearson Creek Pirate, with thirty; Field Ch. Pearson Creek Jason, with twenty-two; Field Ch. Pearson Creek Fred, with twenty-two; Field Ch. Pearson Creek Danny, with twenty-one; Field Ch. Pearson Creek Chip, with twenty; and Field Ch. Pearson Creek Farmer, with seven champion get. Carson, Barbarian, and Jason are by Stub, while Nick, Moe, and Piper are by Carson.

Quality bitches are the backbone of any kennel and Pearson Creek has had several. The top producing bitch is Field Ch. Pearson Creek Countess, who is the dam of sixteen champions. Field Ch. Pearson Creek Cajun Queen has twelve, Field Ch. Pearson Creek Melodie has eleven, and Field Ch. B-Line Stubbi has ten. Countess is the dam of Queen, who is the dam of Stub. Melodie and Stubbi are Stub daughters.

Pendleton Beagles take their name from the town in Indiana in which Paul and Helen Jeffrey located their kennel. Field Ch. Pendleton Tonto is a Wind Creek Limbo son out of a Pearson Creek bitch. Another young stud is Field Ch. Pendleton Louie.

Quaker Hill Beagles is owned by J. Carl Lehman and is located in Bannock, Ohio. Thirteen inch winners at this kennel are Field Ch. Watson's Danny Boy and Field Ch. Cook's Carson, already the sire of champions.

Forest Hill, Tennessee, is the home of the kennel of W. C. Richards. His stud dog, Field Ch. French Creek Scooter, is the

Ravenswood Whispering Smith and Ch. Ravenswood Hamlin Harmony winning Best Brace in Show. Owners are Mr. and Mrs. Donald Barnes.

Ch. The Whim's Buckeye, owned by Mrs. A. C. Musladin.

sire of kennel mates Derby Field Ch. Hinton's Sir Watson and Field Ch. Town and Country Black Jack.

River Oaks Beagles is owned by Malcolm Brown of Catawba, North Carolina. Field Ch. River Oaks Ronnie, a Carson son, is the sire of sixteen champions, including Field Ch. River Oaks Raymond, Field Ch. River Oaks Buttons, and Field Ch. River Oaks Dixie. The young Field Ch. River Oaks Rudy, a son of Field Ch. River Oaks Gail, is already the sire of champions.

The Beagles of Russ-Kill are owned by Russel Kilmer and are kenneled in Lambertsville, New Jersey. Their stud, Derby Field Ch. Pearson Creek Barbin, is the sire of Derby Field Ch. Russ-Kill's Brandy. Another winning kennel mate is Derby Field Ch. Cobby's Butcher Boy.

Harold Smith's kennel is located in Pensacola, Florida. His Field Ch. Rhythm Run Sam is a Wind Creek Limbo son. He is the sire of several champions with others close to the title.

Sunny Hill Beagles is owned by James I. Maddox and is located in Buford, Georgia. Two thirteen inch dogs in this kennel are Field Ch. Sunny Hill Sitting Down Sam and Field Ch. Sunny Hill Scooter.

Sunrize Beagles is owned by Art Fleming of Mars, Pennsylvania. Field Ch. Sunrize Drummer is another Wind Creek Limbo son. He is joined in the kennel by Field Ch. El-Art Piper.

Thunder Run Beagles is located in Flemington, New Jersey, and is owned by Grant Schibilia. A double grandson of Stub, Field Ch. Pearson Creek Pirate, is the sire of thirty champions. Field Ch. Hollow Creek Limbo, a Wind Creek Limbo son, also stands at stud in this kennel.

James B. Tignor, Jr., established his kennel in Nashville, Tennessee. The thirteen inch stud force represents three generations of Beagle winners. Field Ch. Pearson Creek Chip is the sire of twenty champions. His son Field Ch. Pearson Creek Blue Chip is the sire of Field Ch. Glencliff Tommy. Tommy is a double grandson of Pearson Creek Chip.

Cliff Troxell located his kennel in Auburn, Indiana. His stud force is represented by Field Ch. Bil-Bob-Kin's Bozo, Field Ch. Pearson Creek Cody, and Field Ch. Indians Buck III.

Walk-A-Line Kennel of William and Peggy Givens is located in Natchez, Mississippi. Field Ch. Walk-A-Line Lil Abner is a Wind Creek Limbo son. A half-brother is Field Ch. Walk-A-Line Patrick. They are both out of Walk-a-Line Vickie.

Westbank Beagles of Bridge City, Louisiana, are owned by Joe Hymel. Field Ch. Westbank Limbo and Field Ch. Westbank Tiny Tim are both Limbo sons. Limbo is the sire of sixteen champions and Tim has six.

Jesse and John Wilson of Grass Lake, Michigan, own two Limbo sons: Field Ch. War Eagle Ace and Field Ch. Jolly Run Wiki-Wiki. Ace is the sire of seven champions.

Yellow Pine Beagles of Warren and Martha Smith of Montgomery, Alabama, are the owners of Field Ch. Wind Creek Limbo. Limbo is among the all-time great sires with just under one hundred field champion get. He is joined in the kennel by two sons, Field Ch. Forrest Range Limbo and Field Ch. Smoke Pole Limbo.

English Ch. Rossut Daffodil, owned by Catherine G. Sutton.

English Ch. Rossut Triumphant, the top winning Beagle in England, owned by Catherine G. Sutton.

Rozavel Diamond Ring, owned by Thelma Gray.

English Ch. Rossut Foreman, owned by Catherine G. Sutton.

The Beagle in Other Countries

The English Kennel Club, founded in 1873, is the oldest such organization in the world. The second oldest is The American Kennel Club, founded in 1884. Other early organizations are the Kennel Club of Denmark, 1887; the Kennel Club of Sweden *(Svenska Kennel Klubben)*, 1888; and the Canadian Kennel Club, 1888; The Finnish Kennel Club, 1889; and the Norwegian Kennel Club, 1889. More recent clubs are: the French Kennel Club *(Société Centrale Canine)*, the German Kennel Club *(Verband für das Deutsche Hundewesen)*, the Spanish Central Society *(Real Sociedad Central de Fomento de las Razas Caninas en Espana)*, the New Zealand Kennel Club, the Portuguese Kennel Club *(Club Portuguese de Canicultura)*, and the Australian National Kennel Council, established in 1958. This latter organization serves as a central unit for the clubs of the various states in Australia. The Scandinavian Kennel Union, founded in 1953, serves the same function for the four Scandinavian countries.

In Germany the Beagle *(Brake)* is in Group I, *Jadghundrassen,* or the Sporting-Hound Dogs. Group II is the *Hetzhundrassen,* or Sporting-Stag Hound Dogs. The Beagle is, according to the meaning of the German word, a Trailing Scent Hound. In spite of the fact that the word Beagle may be a corruption of the medieval French word *Bégueule,* the present-day French word is Beagle. The Beagle in France is in Group III, *Chiens Courants,* or Running Dogs. France divides its 130 recognized breeds into eight Groups. The Germans divide their sixty-six breeds into five Groups. Spain lists fifteen breeds, divided into four Groups, and places the Beagle *(Sabueso)* in the Track Hound Group. In Sweden the Beagle is one of seventy-eight breeds and is classified as *Stövare,* or Hound. It is interesting to note that in the jungles of two different countries on opposite sides of the globe the Beagle is used as a cat-tracking dog. Both in Ceylon and in Venezuela the Beagle is hunted in packs to track down the jaguar and the leopard.

The English Kennel Club divides the entries for both dogs and bitches into eight classes. They are: Special Puppy, for dogs six to nine months; Puppy, six to twelve months; Junior, six to eighteen months; Maiden, for dogs that have never won a first prize; Novice, for dogs that have not won a Challenge Certificate nor more than three first prizes; Graduate, for dogs that have not won a Challenge Certificate nor more than four first prizes; Open, for any dog; Veteran, for dogs seven years or older. The English Kennel Club sponsors both open and championship shows. Challenge Certificates are only available at the championship shows.

The German Kennel Club sponsors a World Championship show. Breed winners here can earn in a single show the titles of German Champion, World Champion, and the *Certificat d'Aptitude au Championat Internationale* (CACIB) award. Each dog is given one of the following five ratings: Excellent, Very Good, Good, Satisfactory, and Unsatisfactory.

The German Beagle Club, young by comparison to specialty clubs in some other countries, sponsors its own show. This club is dedicated to the improvement of the breed and will not accept for membership anyone who is in commercial Beagles. This philosophical opposition to puppy mills is highly commendable.

In England the Beagle does not enjoy the popularity that he does in the United States. In 1969 he ranked sixteenth among all breeds but had slipped to twenty-first place by 1972. Both the Afghan and the Basset are now ahead of him in the Hound Group. Registrations in 1969 were 3,979; in 1970, 3,445; 1971, 3,209; and in 1972, 3,033.

The Bravae Beagle Kennel is located in Lincolnshire and is owned by Mrs. G. M. Clayton and Miss Pat Clayton. There are more than three dozen champions carrying the Bravae title. Among the many title holders are: Ch. Bravae Paigan, Ch. Bravae Vesper, Ch. Bravae Statute, and Ch. Bravae Garland. Bravae Vella is the winner of a Best-in-Show award.

Mrs. M. A. Gibson and Mrs. P. J. Parker are the owners of Cornevon Beagle Kennel, located in Hertfordshire. The quality of their breeding program is indicated by their several generations of home-bred champions. Ch. Cornevon Pensive is the dam of Ch. Cornevon Garland and two other champions. Ch. Cornevon Garland, in turn, is also the dam of three champions. Other banner winners from this kennel are Ch. Cornevon Pirouette and Ch. Cornevon Sandpiper.

Wolverhampton is the location of the Cannybuff Kennel of Mrs. E. Crowther-Davies. Ch. Cannybuff Clipper earned fourteen Challenge Certificates in his show career. Other Beagles carrying the kennel banner are Ch. Cannybuff Curry, Ch. Cannybuff Bravae Playful, and Ch. Cannybuff Cider.

Mrs. Dorothy Marco operates her Deaconfield Beagle Kennel in Berkshire. Her Ch. Deaconfield Rampage is one of the leading sires. He has seven champion get. Two of his latest winners are Ch. Houndswood Havoc, owned by Dr. D. Heywood, and Ch. Crestamere Kerry Dancer, owned by Mrs. Wyn Mahonys. Kerry Dancer is a home-bred out of Mrs. Mahony's Ch. Crestamere Orchid. Havoc, in addition to being a bench champion, also holds a working certificate, which is equivalent to an obedience title in the United States. Among the other winners of Mrs. Marco are Ch. Deaconfield Random and Ch. Deaconfield Renown.

Many Beagles have earned their titles under the Dialynne Kennel banner of Mrs. M. M. Spavin of Lincolnshire. Ch. Dialynne Gamble has won seventeen Challenge Certificates and was a Best-in-Show winner at the Beagle Association Championship Show. Ch. Dialynne Huntsman earned his final certificate at a specialty show. Other banner winners are Ch. Dialynne Nettle, Ch. Dialynne Shadow, and Ch. Dialynne Ponder. The latter is the sire of four champions. Mr. Jack Peden of Gateside Kennels showed Dialynne Strathdene Fettle to the title in both England and Ireland. This dog also earned a Specialty Best-in-Show award.

Mrs. Eleanor Bothwell of Ayrshire, Scotland, has exported a number of show dogs. She has finished for herself the stud dog Ch. Korwin Monitor.

Raimex Kennel of Oxford is operated by D. Brown. Ch. Raimex Talley is the standard bearer for this kennel, with twelve Challenge Certificates. Another winner is Raimex Wager.

James F. G. Hall of Surrey is the owner of the Redgate Beagle Kennel. Among his winning dogs are Ch. Redgate Marquis and Redgate Gaiety.

The Rozavel Kennel of Mrs. Thelma Gray is located in Pirbright, Surrey. Mrs. Gray imported her foundation stock from the United States. Among these dogs are American Ch. Renoca's Best Showman, American Ch. Rozavel Elsy's Diamond Jerry, American Ch. Rozavel Ritter's Sweet Sue, and American Ch. Rozavel Ritter's Miss Babe. From this stock Mrs. Gray bred such English winners as Ch. Rozavel Earring, Ch. Rozavel Texan Starlet, and Ch. Rozavel Ziwi.

Ch. Rozavel Elsy's Diamond Jerry has won the Progeny Class (Stud Dog) at the Beagle Association Championship (Specialty) Show five times, on one occasion having twenty-five of his get en-

Rozavel Blaze, owned by Thelma Gray.

tered in regular class competition. Mrs. Gray has exported dogs to Australia, to New Zealand, and to Germany, where one dog won the title of *Weltjugendsieger* in 1973. In addition to Beagles, Rozavel breeds Chihuahuas, Welsh Corgis, Alsatians, and West Highland White Terriers.

The Rossut Kennel of Mrs. Catherine G. Sutton is located in Camberley, Surrey. This is the top winning Beagle kennel in England and holds the distinction of having won 106 Challenge Certificates with Beagles. Ch. Rossut Triumphant won twenty-three CC's as well as an all-breed Best-in-Show award. A second Best-in-Show winner is Ch. Rossut Gaiety. A Reserve Best-in-Show

English Ch. Rozavel Madison, owned by Thelma Gray.

award was won by Ch. Rossut Foreman, who also won ten CC's and was the top winning dog in 1973. Ch. Rossut Daffodil, a lemon and white, was the top winning bitch in 1972 and won a CC at Crufts in 1973. Other winners are Ch. Rossut Vagabond and Ch. Rossut Bobbin.

Mrs. Sutton's interests in dogs are varied. In addition to Beagles she breeds Boxers, Pointers, Labradors, Norwich Terriers, Pugs, and Yorkshire Terriers. Mrs. Sutton is also a licensed judge and has had assignments in many countries, including the United States.

There are a number of other breeders and owners who are currently showing dogs that are doing significant winning. Mrs. M. Furst-Danielson owns the 1973 Crufts winner, Ch. Southcourt Wembury Fiddler. In addition to winning the breed at Crufts, he went on to place second in the Hound Group. He now has sixteen Challenge Certificates. Mrs. W. F. G. Hayes has a winner in Ch. Beston Harmony, a bitch. At Letton Kennels in Northampton Mrs. Beck has finished Ch. Letton Americano. Mrs. Annette S. Mawson's Lancashire Larkholme Kennel owns the dog Ch. Larkholme Andima Classic Major. Ch. Webline Holly is owned by the Webline Kennel of Mr. and Mrs. D. J. Webster and Mrs. D. George of Hampshire. Mrs. R. A. MacDonald of Hertfordshire represents her Rosebrooke Kennel with the bitch Ch. Rosebrooke Rebel. Mr. and Mrs. Leonard Priestly of Lancashire have campaigned Ch. Pinewood Crumpet under their Pinewood banner.

A number of Beagles have been exported from England to other countries around the world, where they are bringing fame to their home kennel. Mrs. H. G. Lansbergen of Schiplinden, Holland, has campaigned English Ch. Dialynne Storm to titles in Holland and Luxembourg as well as to the title of World Champion with CAB and CACIB. Dialynne Imp, a kennel mate, also has the title of World Champion. Ch. Pippative Vanicoro Viking, exported to Mrs. M. T. Spafford, went Best in Show in Portugal.

Rossut Kennel is represented in Australia with Ch. Rossut Colinbar Phantom, who has accumulated twenty-four Challenge Certificates. Rozavel Kennel is represented in Ceylon with Ch. Rozavel Colorado and in New Zealand with Ch. Rozavel Kiwi. In Italy, Ch. Korwin Candida, CACIB, a Scottish import, won a Hound Group and was Reserve Best in Show in 1973. At a Championship Show in Helsinki, Finland, in 1973, the English export Barrister of Beacott, CACIB, won a CC and was Reserve Best in Show.

Head study of Ch. Page Mill Wildfire, owned by Dr. and
Mrs. A. C. Musladin.

Head study of Ch. The Whim's Touch-Me-Not, owned by
Mrs. A. C. Musladin.

Manners for
the Family Dog

Although each dog has personality quirks and idiosyncrasies that set him apart as an individual, dogs in general have two characteristics that can be utilized to advantage in training. The first is the dog's strong desire to please, which has been built up through centuries of association with man. The second lies in the innate quality of the dog's mentality. It has been proved conclusively that while dogs have reasoning power, their learning ability is based on a direct association of cause and effect, so that they willingly repeat acts that bring pleasant results and discontinue acts that bring unpleasant results. Hence, to take fullest advantage of a dog's abilities, the trainer must make sure the dog understands a command, and then reward him when he obeys and correct him when he does wrong.

Commands should be as short as possible and should be repeated in the same way, day after day. Saying "Heel," one day, and "Come here and heel," the next will confuse the dog. *Heel, sit, stand, stay, down,* and *come* are standard terminology, and are preferable for a dog that may later be given advanced training.

Tone of voice is important, too. For instance, a coaxing tone helps cajole a young puppy into trying something new. Once an exercise is mastered, commands given in a firm, matter-of-fact voice give the dog confidence in his own ability. Praise, expressed in an exuberant tone will tell the dog quite clearly that he has earned his master's approval. On the other hand, a firm "No" indicates with equal clarity that he has done wrong.

Rewards for good performance may consist simply of praising lavishly and petting the dog, although many professional trainers use bits of food as rewards. Tidbits are effective only if the dog is hungry, of course. And if you smoke, you must be sure to wash your hands before each training session, for the odor of nicotine is repulsive to dogs. On the hands of a heavy smoker, the odor of nicotine may be so strong that the dog is unable to smell the tidbit.

Correction for wrong-doing should be limited to repeating "No," in a scolding tone of voice or to confining the dog to his bed. Spanking or striking the dog is taboo—particularly using sticks, which might cause injury, but the hand should never be used either. For field training as well as some obedience work, the hand is used to signal the dog. Dogs that have been punished by slapping have a tendency to cringe whenever they see a hand raised and consequently do not respond promptly when the owner's intent is not to punish but to signal.

Some trainers recommend correcting the dog by whacking him with a rolled-up newspaper. The idea is that the newspaper will not injure the dog but that the resulting noise will condition the dog to avoid repeating the act that seemingly caused the noise. Many authorities object to this type of correction, for it may result in the dog's becoming "noise-shy"—a decided disadvantage with show dogs which must maintain poise in adverse, often noisy, situations. "Noise-shyness" is also an unfortunate reaction in field dogs, since it may lead to gun-shyness.

To be effective, correction must be administered immediately, so that in the dog's mind there is a direct connection between his act and the correction. You can make voice corrections under almost any circumstances, but you must never call the dog to you and then correct him, or he will associate the correction with the fact that he has come and will become reluctant to respond. If the dog is at a distance and doing something he shouldn't, go to him and scold him while he is still involved in wrong-doing. If this is impossible, ignore the offense until he repeats it and you can correct him properly.

Especially while a dog is young, he should be watched closely and stopped before he gets into mischief. All dogs need to do a certain amount of chewing, so to prevent your puppy's chewing something you value, provide him with his own rubber balls and toys. Never allow him to chew cast-off slippers and then expect him to differentiate between cast-off items and those you value. Nylon stockings, wooden articles, and various other items may cause intestinal obstructions if the dog chews and swallows them, and death may result. So it is essential that the dog be permitted to chew only on bones or rubber toys.

Serious training for obedience should not be started until a dog is a year old. But basic training in house manners should begin the day the puppy enters his new home. A puppy should never be given the run of the house but should be confined to a box or small pen except for play periods when you can devote full attention to him. The first thing to teach the dog is his name, so that whenever he hears it, he will immediately come to attention. Whenever you are near his box, talk to him, using his name repeatedly. During play periods, talk to him, pet him, and handle him, for he must be conditioned so he will not object to being handled by a veterinarian, show judge, or family friend. As the dog investigates his surroundings, watch him carefully and if he tries something he shouldn't, reprimand him with a scolding "No!" If he repeats the offense, scold him and confine him to his box, then praise him. Discipline must be prompt, consistent, and always followed with praise. Never tease the dog, and never allow others to do so. Kindness and understanding are essential to a pleasant, mutually rewarding relationship.

When the puppy is two to three months old, secure a flat, narrow leather collar and have him start wearing it (never use a harness, which will encourage tugging and pulling). After a week or so, attach a light leather lead to the collar during play sessions and let the puppy walk around, dragging the lead behind him. Then start holding the end of the lead and coaxing the puppy to come to you. He will then be fully accustomed to collar and lead when you start taking him outside while he is being housebroken.

Housebreaking can be accomplished in a matter of approximately two weeks provided you wait until the dog is mature enough to have some control over bodily functions. This is usually at about four months. Until that time, the puppy should spend most of his day confined to his penned area, with the floor covered with several thicknesses of newspapers so that he may relieve himself when necessary without damage to floors.

Either of two methods works well in housebreaking—the choice depending upon where you live. If you live in a house with a readily accessible yard, you will probably want to train the puppy from the beginning to go outdoors. If you live in an apartment without easy access to a yard, you may decide to train him first to relieve himself on newspapers and then when he has learned control, to teach the puppy to go outdoors.

If you decide to train the puppy by taking him outdoors, arrange some means of confining him indoors where you can watch him closely—in a small penned area, or tied to a short lead (five or six feet). Dogs are naturally clean animals, reluctant to soil their quarters, and confining the puppy to a limited area will encourage him to avoid making a mess.

A young puppy must be taken out often, so watch your puppy closely and if he indicates he is about to relieve himself, take him out at once. If he has an accident, scold him and take him out so he will associate the act of going outside with the need to relieve himself. Always take the puppy out within an hour after meals—preferably to the same place each time—and make sure he relieves himself before you return him to the house. Restrict his water for two hours before bedtime and take him out just before you retire for the night. Then, as soon as you wake in the morning, take him out again.

For paper training, set aside a particular room and cover a large area of the floor with several thicknesses of newspapers. Confine the dog on a short leash and each time he relieves himself, remove the soiled papers and replace them with clean ones.

As his control increases, gradually decrease the paper area, leaving part of the floor bare. If he uses the bare floor, scold him mildly and put him on the papers, letting him know that there is where he is to relieve himself. As he comes to understand the idea, increase the bare area until papers cover only space equal to approximately two full newspaper sheets. Keep him using the papers, but begin taking him on a leash to the street at the times of day that he habitually relieves himself. Watch him closely when he is indoors and at the first sign that he needs to go, take him outdoors. Restrict his water for two hours before bedtime, but if necessary, permit him to use the papers before you retire for the night.

Using either method, the puppy will be housebroken in an amazingly short time. Once he has learned control he will need to relieve himself only four or five times a day.

Informal obedience training, started at the age of about six to eight months, will provide a good background for any advanced training you may decide to give your dog later. The collar most

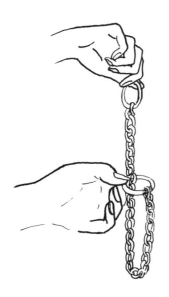

effective for training is the metal chain-link variety. The correct size for your dog will be about one inch longer than the measurement around the largest part of his head. The chain must be slipped through one of the rings so the collar forms a loop. The collar should be put on with the loose ring at the right of the dog's neck, the chain attached to it coming over the neck and through the holding ring, rather than under the neck. Since the dog is to be at your left during most of the training, this makes the collar most effective.

The leash should be attached to the loose ring, and should be either webbing or leather, six feet long and a half inch to a full inch wide. When you want your dog's attention, or wish to correct him, give a light, quick pull on the leash, which will momentarily tighten the collar about the neck. Release the pressure instantly, and the correction will have been made. If the puppy is already accustomed to a leather collar, he will adjust easily to the training collar. But before you start training sessions, practice walking with the dog until he responds readily when you increase tension on the leash.

Set aside a period of fifteen minutes, once or twice a day, for regular training sessions, and train in a place where there will be no distractions. Teach only one exercise at a time, making sure the dog has mastered it before going on to another. It will probably take at least a week for the dog to master each exercise. As training progresses, start each session by reviewing exercises the dog has already learned, then go on to the new exercise for a period of concerted practice. When discipline is required, make the correction immediately, and always praise the dog after corrections as well as when he obeys promptly. During each session stick strictly to business. Afterwards, take time to play with the dog.

The first exercise to teach is heeling. Have the dog at your left and hold the leash as shown in the illustration on the preceding page. Start walking, and just as you put your foot forward for the first step, say your dog's name to get his attention, followed by the command, "Heel!" Simultaneously, pull on the leash lightly. As you walk, try to keep the dog at your left side, with his head alongside your left leg. Pull on the leash as necessary to urge him forward or back, to right or left, but keep him in position. Each time you pull on the leash, say "Heel!" and praise the dog lavishly. When the dog heels properly in a straight line, start making circles, turning corners, etc.

Once the dog has learned to heel well, start teaching the "sit." Each time you stop while heeling, command "Sit!" The dog will be at your left, so use your left hand to press on his rear and guide him to a sitting position, while you use the leash in your right hand to keep his head up. Hold him in position for a few moments while you praise him, then give the command to heel. Walk a few steps, stop, and repeat the procedure. Before long he will automatically sit whenever you stop. You can then teach the dog to "sit" from any position.

When the dog will sit on command without correction, he is ready to learn to stay until you release him. Simply sit him, command "Stay!" and hold him in position for perhaps half a minute, repeating "Stay," if he attempts to stand. You can release him by saying "O.K." Gradually increase the time until he will stay on command for three or four minutes.

The "stand-stay" should also be taught when the dog is on leash. While you are heeling, stop and give the command "Stand!" Keep the dog from sitting by quickly placing your left arm under him, immediately in front of his right hind leg. If he continues to try to sit, don't scold him but start up again with the heel command, walk a few steps, and stop again, repeating the stand command and preventing the dog from sitting. Once the dog has mastered the stand, teach him to stay by holding him in position and repeating the word "Stay!"

The "down stay" will prove beneficial in many situations, but especially if you wish to take your dog in the car without confining him to a crate. To teach the "down," have the dog sitting at your side with collar and leash on. If he is a large dog, step forward with the leash in your hand and turn so you face him. Let the leash touch the floor, then step over it with your right foot so it is under the instep of your shoe. Grasping the leash low down with both hands, slowly pull up, saying, "Down!" Hold the leash taut until the dog goes down. Once he responds well, teach the dog to stay in the down position (the down-stay), using the same method as for the sit- and stand-stays.

To teach small dogs the "down," another method may be used. Have the dog sit at your side, then kneel beside him. Reach across his back with your left arm, and take hold of his left front leg close to the body. At the same time, with your right hand take hold of his right front leg close to his body. As you command "Down!" gently lift the legs and place the dog in the down position. Release your hold on his legs and slide your left hand onto his back, repeating, "Down, stay," while keeping him in position.

The "come" is taught when the dog is on leash and heeling. Simply walk along, then suddenly take a step backward, saying "Come!" Pull the leash as you give the command and the dog will turn and follow you. Continue walking backward, repeatedly saying "Come," and tightening the leash if necessary.

Once the dog has mastered the exercises while on leash, try taking the leash off and going through the same routine, beginning with the heeling exercise. If the dog doesn't respond promptly, he needs review with the leash on. But patience and persistence will be rewarded, for you will have a dog you can trust to respond promptly under all conditions.

Even after they are well trained, dogs sometimes develop bad habits that are hard to break. Jumping on people is a common habit, and all members of the family must assist if it is to be broken. If the dog is a large or medium breed, take a step forward and raise your knee just as he starts to jump on you. As your knee strikes the dog's chest, command "Down!" in a scolding voice. When a small dog jumps on you, take both front paws in your hands, and, while talking in a pleasant tone of voice, step on the dog's back feet just hard enough to hurt them slightly. With either method the dog is taken by surprise and doesn't associate the discomfort with the person causing it.

Occasionally a dog may be too chummy with guests who don't care for dogs. If the dog has had obedience training, simply command "Come!" When he responds, have him sit beside you.

Excessive barking is likely to bring complaints from neighbors, and persistent efforts may be needed to subdue a dog that barks without provocation. To correct the habit, you must be close to the dog when he starts barking. Encircle his muzzle with both hands, hold his mouth shut, and command "Quiet!" in a firm voice. He should soon learn to respond so you can control him simply by giving the command.

Sniffing other dogs is an annoying habit. If the dog is off leash and sniffs other dogs, ignoring your commands to come, he needs to review the lessons on basic behavior. When the dog is on leash, scold him, then pull on the leash, command "Heel," and walk away from the other dog.

A well-trained dog will be no problem if you decide to take him with you when you travel. No matter how well he responds, however, he should never be permitted off leash when you walk him in a strange area. Distractions will be more tempting, and there will be more chance of his being attacked by other dogs. So whenever the dog travels with you, take his collar and leash along—and use them.

Bench Shows

Centuries ago, it was common practice to hold agricultural fairs in conjunction with spring and fall religious festivals, and to these gatherings, cattle, dogs, and other livestock were brought for exchange. As time went on, it became customary to provide entertainment, too. Dogs often participated in such sporting events as bull baiting, bear baiting, and ratting. Then the dog that exhibited the greatest skill in the arena was also the one that brought the highest price when time came for barter or sale. Today, these fairs seem a far cry from our highly organized bench shows and field trials. But they were the forerunners of modern dog shows and played an important role in shaping the development of purebred dogs.

The first organized dog show was held at Newcastle, England, in 1859. Later that same year, a show was held at Birmingham. At both shows dogs were divided into four classes and only Pointers and Setters were entered. In 1860, the first dog show in Germany was held at Apoldo, where nearly one hundred dogs were exhibited and entries were divided into six groups. Interest expanded rapidly, and by the time the Paris Exhibition was held in 1878, the dog show was a fixture of international importance.

In the United States, the first organized bench show was held in 1874 in conjunction with the meeting of the Illinois State Sportsmen's Association in Chicago, and all entries were dogs of sporting breeds. Although the show was a rather casual affair, interest spread quickly. Before the end of the year, shows were held in Oswego, New York, Mineola, Long Island, and Memphis, Tennessee. And the latter combined a bench show with the first organized field trial ever held in the United States. In January 1875, an all-breed show (the first in the United States) was held at Detroit, Michigan. From then on, interest increased rapidly, though rules were not always uniform, for there was no organization through which to coordinate activities until September 1884

Benching area at Westminster Kennel Club Show.

Judging for Best in Show at Westminster Kennel Club Show.

when The American Kennel Club was founded. Now the largest dog registering organization in the world, the A.K.C. is an association of several hundred member clubs—all breed, specialty, field trial, and obedience groups—each represented by a delegate to the A.K.C. The several thousand shows and trials held annually in the United States do much to stimulate interest in breeding to produce better looking, sounder, purebred dogs. For breeders, shows provide a means of measuring the merits of their work as compared with accomplishments of other breeders. For hundreds of thousands of dog fanciers, they provide an absorbing hobby.

For both spectators and participating owners, field trials constitute a fascinating demonstration of dogs competing under actual hunting conditions, where emphasis is on excellence of performance. The trials are sponsored by clubs or associations of persons interested in hunting dogs. Trials for Pointing breeds, Dachshunds, Retrievers, Spaniels, and Beagles are under the jurisdiction of The American Kennel Club and information concerning such activities is published in "Pure Bred Dogs—American Kennel Gazette." Trials for Bird Dogs are run by rules and regulations of the Amateur Field Trial Clubs of America and information concerning them is published in "The American Field."

All purebred dogs of recognized breeds may be registered with The American Kennel Club and those of hunting breeds may also be registered with The American Field. Dogs that have won championships both in the field and in bench shows are known as dual champions.

At bench (or conformation) shows, dogs are rated comparatively on their physical qualities (or conformation) in accordance with breed Standards which have been approved by The American Kennel Club. Characteristics such as size, coat, color, placement of eye or ear, general soundness, etc., are the basis for selecting the best dog in a class. Only purebred dogs are eligible to compete and if the show is one where points toward a championship are to be awarded, a dog must be at least six months old.

Bench shows are of various types. An all-breed show has classes for all of the breeds recognized by The American Kennel Club as well as a Miscellaneous Class for breeds not recognized, such as the Australian Cattle Dog, the Ibizan Hound, the Spinoni Italiani, the Tibetan Terrier, etc. A sanctioned match is an informal meeting where dogs compete but not for championship points. A specialty show is confined to a single breed. Other shows may restrict entries to champions of record, to American-bred dogs, etc. Competition for Junior Showmanship or for Best Brace, Best Team, or Best Local Dog may be included. Also, obedience competition is held in conjunction with many bench shows.

The term "bench show" is somewhat confusing in that shows of this type may be either "benched" or "unbenched." At the former, each dog is assigned an individual numbered stall where he must remain throughout the show except for times when he is being judged, groomed, or exercised. At unbenched shows, no stalls are provided and dogs are kept in their owners' cars or in crates when not being judged.

A show where a dog is judged for conformation actually constitutes an elimination contest. To begin with, the dogs of a single breed compete with others of their breed in one of the regular classes: Puppy, Novice, Bred by Exhibitor, American-Bred, or Open, and, finally, Winners, where the top dogs of the preceding five classes meet. The next step is the judging for Best of Breed (or Best of Variety of Breed). Here the Winners Dog and Winners Bitch (or the dog named Winners if only one prize is awarded) compete with any champions that are entered, together with any undefeated dogs that have competed in additional non-regular classes. The dog named Best of Breed (or Best of Variety of Breed), then goes on to compete with the other Best of Breed winners in his Group. The dogs that win in Group competition then compete for the final and highest honor, Best in Show.

When the Winners Class is divided by sex, championship points are awarded the Winners Dog and Winners Bitch. If the Winners Class is not divided by sex, championship points are awarded the dog or bitch named Winners. The number of points awarded varies, depending upon such factors as the number of dogs competing, the Schedule of Points established by the Board of Directors of the A.K.C., and whether the dog goes on to win Best of Breed, the Group, and Best in Show.

In order to become a champion, a dog must win fifteen points, including points from at least two major wins—that is, at least two shows where three or more points are awarded. The major wins must be under two different judges, and one or more of the remaining points must be won under a third judge. The most points ever awarded at a show is five and the least is one, so, in order to become

Junior Showmanship Competition at Westminster Kennel Club Show.

a champion, a dog must be exhibited and win in at least three shows, and usually he is shown many times before he wins his championship.

"Pure Bred Dogs—American Kennel Gazette" and other dog magazines contain lists of forthcoming shows, together with names and addresses of sponsoring organizations to which you may write for entry forms and information relative to fees, closing dates, etc. Before entering your dog in a show for the first time, you should familiarize yourself with the regulations and rules governing competition. You may secure such information from The American Kennel Club or from a local dog club specializing in your breed. It is essential that you also familiarize yourself with the A.K.C. approved Standard for your breed so you will be fully aware of characteristics worthy of merit as well as those considered faulty, or possibly even serious enough to disqualify the dog from competition. For instance, monorchidism (failure of one testicle to descend) and cryptorchidism (failure of both testicles to descend) are disqualifying faults in all breeds.

If possible, you should first attend a show as a spectator and observe judging procedures from ringside. It will also be helpful to join a local breed club and to participate in sanctioned matches before entering an all-breed show.

The dog should be equipped with a narrow leather show lead and a show collar—never an ornamented or spiked collar. For benched shows, a metal-link bench chain will be needed to fasten the dog to the bench. For unbenched shows, the dog's crate should be taken along so that he may be confined in comfort when he is not appearing in the ring. A dog should never be left in a car with all the windows closed. In hot weather the temperature will become unbearable in a very short time. Heat exhaustion may result from even a short period of confinement, and death may ensue.

Food and water dishes will be needed, as well as a supply of the food and water to which the dog is accustomed. Brushes and combs are also necessary, so that you may give the dog's coat a final grooming after you arrive at the show.

Familiarize yourself with the schedule of classes ahead of time, for the dog must be fed and exercised and permitted to relieve himself, and any last-minute grooming completed before his class is called. Both you and the dog should be ready to enter the ring unhurriedly. A good deal of skill in conditioning, training, and handling is required if a dog is to be presented properly. And it is essential that the handler himself be composed, for a jittery handler will transmit his nervousness to his dog.

Once the class is assembled in the ring, the judge will ask that the dogs be paraded in line, moving counter-clockwise in a circle. If you have trained your dog well, you will have no difficulty controlling him in the ring, where he must change pace quickly and gracefully and walk and trot elegantly and proudly with head erect. The show dog must also stand quietly for inspection, posing like a statue for several minutes while the judge observes his structure in detail, examines teeth, feet, coat, etc. When the judge calls your dog forward for individual inspection, do not attempt to converse, but answer any questions he may ask.

As the judge examines the class, he measures each dog against the ideal described in the Standard, then measures the dogs against each other in a comparative sense and selects for first place the dog that comes closest to conforming to the Standard for its breed. If your dog isn't among the winners, don't grumble. If he places first, don't brag loudly. For a bad loser is disgusting, but a poor winner is insufferable.

Obedience Competition

For hundreds of years, dogs have been used in England and Germany in connection with police and guard work, and their working potential has been evaluated through tests devised to show agility, strength, and courage. Organized training has also been popular with English and German breeders for many years, although it was first practiced primarily for the purpose of training large breeds in aggressive tactics.

There was little interest in obedience training in the United States until 1933 when Mrs. Whitehouse Walker returned from England and enthusiastically introduced the sport. Two years later, Mrs. Walker persuaded The American Kennel Club to approve organized obedience activities and to assume jurisdiction over obedience rules. Since then, interest has increased at a phenomenal rate, for obedience competition is not only a sport the average spectator can follow readily, but also a sport for which the average owner can train his own dog easily. Obedience competition is suitable for all breeds. Furthermore, there is no limit to the number of dogs that may win in competition, for each dog is scored individually on the basis of a point rating system.

The dog is judged on his response to certain commands, and if he gains a high enough score in three successive trials under different judges, he wins an obedience degree. Degrees awarded are "C.D."— Companion Dog; "C.D.X."—Companion Dog Excellent; and "U.D." —Utility Dog. A fourth degree, the "T.D.," or Tracking Dog degree, may be won at any time and tests for it are held apart from dog shows. The qualifying score is a minimum of 170 points out of a possible total of 200, with no score in any one exercise less than 50% of the points allotted.

Since obedience titles are progressive, earlier titles (with the exception of the tracking degree) are dropped as a dog acquires the next higher degree. If an obedience title is gained in another country in addition to the United States, that fact is signified by the word "International," followed by the title.

Trials for obedience trained dogs are held at most of the larger bench shows, and obedience training clubs are to be found in almost

111

all communities today. Information concerning forthcoming trials and lists of obedience training clubs are included regularly in "Pure Bred Dogs—American Kennel Gazette"—and other dog magazines. Pamphlets containing rules and regulations governing obedience competition are available upon request from The American Kennel Club, 51 Madison Avenue, New York, N.Y. 10010. Rules are revised occasionally, so if you are interested in participating in obedience competition, you should be sure your copy of the regulations is current.

All dogs must comply with the same rules, although in broad jump, high jump, and bar jump competition, the jumps are adjusted to the size of the breed. Classes at obedience trials are divided into Novice (A and B), Open (A and B), and Utility (which may be divided into A and B, at the option of the sponsoring club and with the approval of The American Kennel Club).

The Novice class is for dogs that have not won the title Companion Dog. In Novice A, no person who has previously handled a dog that has won a C.D. title in the obedience ring at a licensed or member trial, and no person who has regularly trained such a dog, may enter or handle a dog. The handler must be the dog's owner or a member of the owner's immediate family. In Novice B, dogs may be handled by the owner or any other person.

The Open A class is for dogs that have won the C.D. title but have not won the C.D.X. title. Obedience judges and licensed handlers may not enter or handle dogs in this class. Each dog must be handled by the owner or by a member of his immediate family. The Open B class is for dogs that have won the title C.D. or C.D.X. A dog may continue to compete in this class after it has won the title U.D. Dogs in this class may be handled by the owner or any other person.

The Utility class is for dogs that have won the title C.D.X. Dogs that have won the title U.D. may continue to compete in this class, and dogs may be handled by the owner or any other person. Provided the A.K.C. approves, a club may choose to divide the Utility class into Utility A and Utility B. When this is done, the Utility A class is for dogs that have won the title C.D.X. and have not won the title U.D. Obedience judges and licensed handlers may not enter or handle dogs in this class. All other dogs that are eligible for the Utility class but not eligible for Utility A may be entered in Utility B.

Novice competition includes such exercises as heeling on and off lead, the stand for examination, coming on recall, and the long sit and the long down.

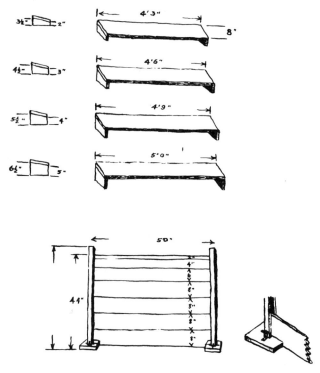

Broad jump and solid hurdle.

In Open competition, the dog must perform such exercises as heeling free, the drop on recall, and the retrieve on the flat and over the high jump. Also, he must execute the broad jump, and the long sit and long down.

In the Utility class, competition includes scent discrimination, the directed retrieve, the signal exercise, directed jumping, and the group examination.

Tracking is the most difficult test. It is always done out-of-doors, of course, and, for obvious reasons, cannot be held at a dog show. The dog must follow a scent trail that is about a quarter mile in length. He is also required to find a scent object (glove, wallet, or other article) left by a stranger who has walked the course to lay down the scent. The dog is required to follow the trail a half to two hours after the scent is laid.

An ideal way to train a dog for obedience competition is to join an obedience class or a training club. In organized class work, beginners' classes cover pretty much the same exercises as those

113

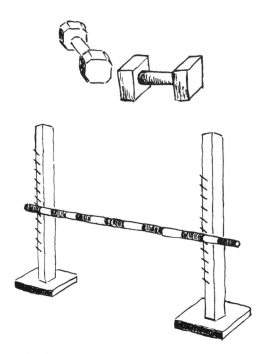

Dumbbells and bar jump.

described in the chapter on training. However, through class work you will develop greater precision than is possible in training your dog by yourself. Amateur handlers often cause the dog to be penalized, for if the handler fails to abide by the rules, it is the dog that suffers the penalty. A common infraction of the rules is using more than one signal or command where regulations stipulate only one may be used. Classwork will help eliminate such errors, which the owner may make unconsciously if he is working alone. Working with a class will also acquaint both dog and handler with ring procedure so that obedience trials will not present unforeseen problems.

Thirty or forty owners and dogs often comprise a class, and exercises are performed in unison, with individual instruction provided if it is required. The procedure followed in training—in fact, even wording of various commands—may vary from instructor to instructor. Equipment used will vary somewhat, also, but will usually include a training collar and leash such as those shown on page 109, a long line, a dumbbell, and a jumping stick.

The latter may be a short length of heavy doweling or a broom handle and both it and the dumbbell are usually painted white for increased visibility.

A bitch in season must never be taken to a training class, so before enrolling a female dog, you should determine whether she may be expected to come into season before classes are scheduled to end. If you think she will, it is better to wait and enroll her in a later course, rather than start the course and then miss classes for several weeks.

In addition to the time devoted to actual work in class, the dog must have regular, daily training sessions for practice at home. Before each class or home training session, the dog should be exercised so he will not be highly excited when the session starts, and he must be given an opportunity to relieve himself before the session begins. (Should he have an accident during the class, it is your responsibility to clean up after him.) The dog should be fed several hours before time for the class to begin or else after the class is over—never just before going to class.

If you decide to enter your dog in obedience competition, it is well to enter a small, informal show the first time. Dogs are usually called in the order in which their names appear in the catalog, so as soon as you arrive at the show, acquaint yourself with the schedule. If your dog is not the first to be judged, spend some time at ringside, observing the routine so you will know what to expect when your dog's turn comes.

In addition to collar, leash, and other equipment, you should take your dog's food and water pans and a supply of the food and water to which he is accustomed. You should also take his brushes and combs in order to give him a last-minute brushing before you enter the ring. It is important that the dog look his best even though he isn't to be judged on his appearance.

Before entering the ring, exercise your dog, give him a drink of water, and permit him to relieve himself. Once your dog enters the ring, give him your full attention and be sure to give voice commands distinctly so he will hear and understand, for there will be many distractions at ringside.

Top dogs in Utility Class. This illustrates variety of breeds that compete in obedience.

Genetics

Genetics, the science of heredity, deals with the processes by which physical and mental traits of parents are transmitted to offspring. For centuries, man has been trying to solve these puzzles, but only in the last two hundred years has significant progress been made.

During the eighteenth century, Kölreuter, a German scientist, made revolutionary discoveries concerning plant sexuality and hybridization but was unable to explain just how hereditary processes worked. In the middle of the nineteenth century, Gregor Johann Mendel, an Augustinian monk, experimented with the ordinary garden pea and made other discoveries of major significance. He found that an inherited characteristic was inherited as a complete unit, and that certain characteristics predominated over others. Next, he observed that the hereditary characteristics of each parent are contained in each offspring, even when they are not visible, and that "hidden" characteristics can be transferred without change in their nature to the grandchildren, or even later generations. Finally, he concluded that although heredity contains an element of uncertainty, some things are predictable on the basis of well-defined mathematical laws.

Unfortunately, Mendel's published paper went unheeded, and when he died in 1884 he was still virtually unknown to the scientific world. But other researchers were making discoveries, too. In 1900, three different scientists reported to learned societies that much of their research in hereditary principles had been proved years before by Gregor Mendel and that findings matched perfectly.

Thus, hereditary traits were proved to be transmitted through the chromosomes found in pairs in every living being, one of each pair contributed by the mother, the other by the father. Within each chromosome have been found hundreds of smaller structures, or genes, which are the actual determinants of hereditary characteristics. Some genes are dominant and will be seen in the offspring. Others are recessive and will not be outwardly apparent, yet can be passed on to the offspring to combine with a similar recessive gene of the other parent and thus be seen. Or they may be passed on to the offspring, not be outwardly apparent, but be passed on again to become apparent in a later generation.

Once the genetic theory of inheritance became widely known, scientists began drawing a well-defined line between inheritance and environment. More recent studies show some overlapping of these influences and indicate a combination of the two may be responsible for certain characteristics. For instance, studies have proved that extreme cold increases the amount of black pigment in the skin and hair of the "Himalayan" rabbit, although it has little or no effect on the white or colored rabbit. Current research also indicates that even though characteristics are determined by the genes, some environmental stress occurring at a particular period of pregnancy might cause physical change in the embryo.

Long before breeders had any knowledge of genetics, they practiced one of its most important principles—selective breeding. Experience quickly showed that "like begets like," and by breeding like with like and discarding unlike offspring, the various individual breeds were developed to the point where variations were relatively few. Selective breeding is based on the idea of maintaining the quality of a breed at the highest possible level, while improving whatever defects are prevalent. It requires that only the top dogs in a litter be kept for later breeding, and that inferior specimens be ruthlessly eliminated.

In planning any breeding program, the first requisite is a definite goal—that is, to have clearly in mind a definite picture of the type of dog you wish eventually to produce. To attempt to breed perfection is to approach the problem unrealistically. But if you don't breed for improvement, it is preferable that you not breed at all.

As a first step, you should select a bitch that exemplifies as many of the desired characteristics as possible and mate her with a dog that also has as many of the desired characteristics as possible. If you start with mediocre pets, you will produce mediocre pet puppies. If you decide to start with more than one bitch, all should closely approach the type you desire, since you will

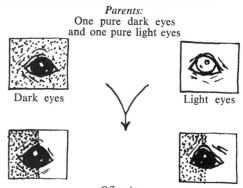

Parents:
One pure dark eyes
and one pure light eyes

Dark eyes   Light eyes

Offspring:
Eyes dark (dominant) with light recessive

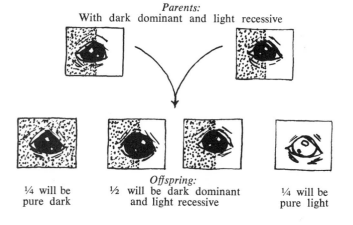

Parents:
With dark dominant and light recessive

¼ will be   *Offspring:*   ¼ will be
pure dark   ½ will be dark dominant   pure light
                and light recessive

The above is a schematic representation of the Mendelian law as it applies to the inheritance of eye color. The law applies in the same way to the inheritance of other physical characteristics.

then stand a better chance of producing uniformly good puppies from all. Breeders often start with a single bitch and keep the best bitches in every succeeding generation.

Experienced breeders look for "prepotency" in breeding stock —that is, the ability of a dog or bitch to transmit traits to most or all of its offspring. While the term is usually used to describe the transmission of good qualities, a dog may also be prepotent in transmitting faults. To be prepotent in a practical sense, a dog must possess many characteristics controlled by dominant genes. If desired characteristics are recessive, they will be apparent in the offspring only if carried by both sire and dam. Prepotent dogs and bitches usually come from a line of prepotent ancestors, but the mere fact that a dog has exceptional ancestors will not necessarily mean that he himself will produce exceptional offspring.

A single dog may sire a tremendous number of puppies, whereas a bitch can produce only a comparatively few litters during her lifetime. Thus, a sire's influence may be very widespread as compared to that of a bitch. But in evaluating a particular litter, it must be remembered that the bitch has had as much influence as has had the dog.

Inbreeding, line-breeding, outcrossing, or a combination of the three are the methods commonly used in selective breeding.

Inbreeding is the mating together of closely related animals, such as father-daughter, mother-son, or brother-sister. Although some breeders insist such breeding will lead to the production of defective individuals, it is through rigid inbreeding that all breeds of dogs have been established. Controlled tests have shown that any harmful effects appear within the first five or ten generations, and that if rigid selection is exercised from the beginning, a vigorous inbred strain will be built up.

Line-breeding is also the mating together of individuals related by family lines. However, matings are made not so much on the basis of the dog's and bitch's relationship to each other, but, instead, on the basis of their relationship to a highly admired ancestor, with a view to perpetuating his qualities. Line-breeding constitutes a long-range program and cannot be accomplished in a single generation.

Outcrossing is the breeding together of two dogs that are unrelated in family lines. Actually, since breeds have been developed through the mating of close relatives, all dogs within any given breed are related to some extent. There are few breedings that are true outcrosses, but if there is no common ancestor within five generations, a mating is usually considered an outcross.

Experienced breeders sometimes outcross for one generation in order to eliminate a particular fault, then go back to inbreeding or line-breeding. Neither the good effects nor the bad effects of outcrossing can be truly evaluated in a single mating, for undesirable recessive traits may be introduced into a strain, yet not show up for several generations. Outcrossing is better left to experienced breeders, for continual outcrossing results in a wide variation in type and great uncertainty as to the results that may be expected.

Two serious defects that are believed heritable—subluxation and orchidism—should be zealously guarded against, and afflicted dogs and their offspring should be eliminated from breeding programs. Subluxation is a condition of the hip joint where the bone of the socket is eroded and the head of the thigh bone is also worn away, causing lameness which becomes progressively more serious until the dog is unable to walk. Orchidism is the failure of one or both testicles to develop and descend properly. When one testicle is involved, the term "monorchid" is used. When both are involved, "cryptorchid" is used. A cryptorchid is almost always sterile, whereas a monorchid is usually fertile. There is evidence that orchidism "runs in families" and that a monorchid transmits the tendency through bitch and male puppies alike.

Through the years, many misconceptions concerning heredity have been perpetuated. Perhaps the one most widely perpetuated is the idea evolved hundreds of years ago that somehow characteristics were passed on through the mixing of the blood of the parents. We still use terminology evolved from that theory when we speak of bloodlines, or describe individuals as full-blooded, despite the fact that the theory was disproved more than a century ago.

Also inaccurate and misleading is any statement that a definite fraction or proportion of an animal's inherited characteristics can be positively attributed to a particular ancestor. Individuals lacking knowledge of genetics sometimes declare that an individual receives half his inherited characteristics from each parent, a quarter from each grandparent, an eighth from each great-grandparent, etc. Thousands of volumes of scientific findings have been published, but no simple way has been found to determine positively which characteristics have been inherited from which ancestors, for the science of heredity is infinitely complex.

Any breeder interested in starting a serious breeding program should study several of the excellent books on canine genetics that are currently available.

Whelping box. Detail at right shows proper side-wall construction which helps keep small puppies confined and provides sheltered nook which to prevent crushing or smothering.

Breeding and Whelping

The breeding life of a bitch begins when she comes into season the first time at the age of about one to two years (depending on what breed she is). Thereafter, she will come in season at roughly six-month intervals, but this, too, is subject to variation. Her maximum fertility builds up from puberty to full maturity and then declines until a state of total sterility is reached in old age. Just when this occurs is hard to determine, for the fact that an older bitch shows signs of being in season doesn't necessarily mean she is still capable of reproducing.

The length of the season varies from eighteen to twenty-one days. The first indication is a pronounced swelling of the vulva with coincidental bleeding (called "showing color") for about the first seven to nine days. The discharge gradually turns to a creamy color, and it is during this phase (estrus), from about the tenth to the fifteenth days, that the bitch is ovulating and is receptive to the male. The ripe, unfertilized ova survive for about seventy-two hours. If fertilization doesn't occur, the ova die and are discharged the next time the bitch comes in season. If fertilization does take place, each ovum attaches itself to the walls of the uterus, a membrane forms to seal it off, and a foetus develops from it.

Following the estrus phase, the bitch is still in season until about the twenty-first day and will continue to be attractive to males, although she will usually fight them off as she did the first few days. Nevertheless, to avoid accidental mating, the bitch must be confined for the entire period. Virtual imprisonment is necessary, for male dogs display uncanny abilities in their efforts to reach a bitch in season.

The odor that attracts the males is present in the bitch's urine, so it is advisable to take her a good distance from the house before permitting her to relieve herself. To eliminate problems completely, your veterinarian can prescribe a preparation that will disguise the odor but will not interfere with breeding when the time is right. Many fanciers use such preparations when exhibiting a bitch and find that nearby males show no interest whatsoever. But it is not advisable to permit a bitch to run loose when she has been given a product of this type, for during estrus she will seek the company of male dogs and an accidental mating may occur.

A potential brood bitch, regardless of breed, should have good bone, ample breadth and depth of ribbing, and adequate room in the pelvic region. Unless a bitch is physically mature—well beyond the puppy stage when she has her first season—breeding should be delayed until her second or a later season. Furthermore, even though it is possible for a bitch to conceive twice a year, she should not be bred oftener than once a year. A bitch that is bred too often will age prematurely and her puppies are likely to lack vigor.

Two or three months before a bitch is to be mated, her physical condition should be considered carefully. If she is too thin, provide a rich, balanced diet plus the regular exercise needed to develop strong, supple muscles. Daily exercise on the lead is as necessary for the too-thin bitch as for the too fat one, although the latter will need more exercise and at a brisker pace, as well as a reduction of food, if she is to be brought to optimum condition. A prospective brood bitch must have had permanent distemper shots as well as rabies vaccination. And a month before her season is due, a veterinarian should examine a stool specimen for worms. If there is evidence of infestation, the bitch should be wormed.

A dog may be used at stud from the time he reaches physical maturity, well on into old age. The first time your bitch is bred, it is well to use a stud that has already proven his ability by having sired other litters. The fact that a neighbor's dog is readily available should not influence your choice, for to produce the best puppies, you must select the stud most suitable from a genetic standpoint.

If the stud you prefer is not going to be available at the time your bitch is to be in season, you may wish to consult your veterinarian concerning medications available for inhibiting the onset of the season. With such preparations, the bitch's season can be delayed indefinitely.

Usually the first service will be successful. However, if it isn't, in most cases an additional service is given free, provided the stud dog is still in the possession of the same owner. If the bitch misses, it may be because her cycle varies widely from normal. Through microscopic examination, a veterinarian can determine exactly when the bitch is entering the estrus phase and thus is likely to conceive.

The owner of the stud should give you a stud-service certificate, providing a four-generation pedigree for the sire and showing the date of mating. The litter registration application is completed only after the puppies are whelped, but it, too, must be signed by the owner of the stud as well as the owner of the bitch. Registration forms may be secured by writing The American Kennel Club.

In normal pregnancy there is usually visible enlargement of the abdomen by the end of the fifth week. By palpation (feeling with the fingers) a veterinarian may be able to distinguish developing puppies as early as three weeks after mating, but it is unwise for a novice to poke and prod, and try to detect the presence of unborn puppies.

The gestation period normally lasts nine weeks, although it may vary from sixty-one to sixty-five days. If it goes beyond sixty-five days from the date of mating, a veterinarian should be consulted.

During the first four or five weeks, the bitch should be permitted her normal amount of activity. As she becomes heavier, she should be walked on the lead, but strenuous running and jumping should be avoided. Her diet should be well balanced (see page 43), and if she should become constipated, small amounts of mineral oil may be added to her food.

A whelping box should be secured about two weeks before the puppies are due, and the bitch should start then to use it as her bed so she will be accustomed to it by the time puppies arrive. Preferably, the box should be square, with each side long enough so that the bitch can stretch out full length and have several inches to spare at either end. The bottom should be padded with an old cotton rug or other material that is easily laundered. Edges of the padding should be tacked to the floor of the box so the puppies will not get caught in it and smother. Once it is obvious labor is about to begin, the padding should be covered with several layers of spread-out newspapers. Then, as papers become soiled, the top layer can be pulled off, leaving the area clean.

Forty-eight to seventy-two hours before the litter is to be whelped, a definite change in the shape of the abdomen will be noted. Instead of looking barrel-shaped, the abdomen will sag pendulously. Breasts usually redden and become enlarged, and milk may be present a day or two before the puppies are whelped. As the time becomes imminent, the bitch will probably scratch and root at her bedding in an effort to make a nest, and will refuse food and ask to be let out every few minutes. But the surest sign is a drop in temperature of two or three degrees about twelve hours before labor begins.

The bitch's abdomen and flanks will contract sharply when labor actually starts, and for a few minutes she will attempt to expel a puppy, then rest for a while and try again. Someone should stay with the bitch the entire time whelping is taking place, and if she appears to be having unusual difficulties, a veterinarian should be called.

Puppies are usually born head first, though some may be born feet first and no difficulty encountered. Each puppy is enclosed in a separate membranous sac that the bitch will remove with her teeth. She will sever the umbilical cord, which will be attached to the soft, spongy afterbirth that is expelled right after the puppy emerges. Usually the bitch eats the afterbirth, so it is necessary to watch and make sure one is expelled for each puppy whelped. If afterbirth is retained, the bitch may develop peritonitis and die.

The dam will lick and nuzzle each newborn puppy until it is warm and dry and ready to nurse. If puppies arrive so close together that she can't take care of them, you can help her by rubbing the puppies dry with a soft cloth. If several have been whelped but the bitch continues to be in labor, all but one should be removed and placed in a small box lined with clean towels and warmed to about seventy degrees. The bitch will be calmer if one puppy is left with her at all times.

Whelping sometimes continues as long as twenty-four hours for a very large litter, but a litter of two or three puppies may be whelped in an hour. When the bitch settles down, curls around the puppies and nuzzles them to her, it usually indicates that all have been whelped.

The bitch should be taken away for a few minutes while you clean the box and arrange clean padding. If her coat is soiled, sponge it clean before she returns to the puppies. Once she is back in the box, offer her a bowl of warm beef broth and a pan of cool water, placing both where she will not have to get up in order to reach them. As soon as she indicates interest in food, give her a generous bowl of chopped meat to which codliver oil and dicalcium phosphate have been added (see page 43).

If inadequate amounts of calcium are provided during the period the puppies are nursing, eclampsia may develop. Symptoms are violent trembling, rapid rise in temperature, and rigidity of muscles. Veterinary assistance must be secured immediately, for death may result in a very short time. Treatment consists of massive doses of calcium gluconate administered intravenously, after which symptoms subside in a miraculously short time.

All puppies are born blind and their eyes open when they are ten to fourteen days old. At first the eyes have a bluish cast and appear weak, and the puppies must be protected from strong light until at least ten days after the eyes open.

To ensure proper emotional development, young dogs should be shielded from loud noises and rough handling. Being lifted by the front legs is painful and may result in permanent injury to the shoulders. So when lifting a puppy, always place one hand under the chest with the forefinger between the front legs, and place the other hand under his bottom.

Sometimes the puppies' nails are so long and sharp that they scratch the bitch's breasts. Since the nails are soft, they can be trimmed with ordinary scissors.

If of a breed that ordinarily has a docked tail, puppies should have their tails shortened when they are three days old. Dewclaws—thumblike appendages appearing on the inside of the legs of some breeds—are removed at the same time. While both are simple procedures, they shouldn't be attempted by amateurs.

In certain breeds it is customary to crop the ears, also. This should be done at about eight weeks of age. Cropping should never be attempted by anyone other than a veterinarian, for it requires use of anesthesia and knowledge of surgical techniques, as well as judgment as to the eventual size of the dog and proportion of ear to be removed so the head will be balanced when the dog is mature.

At about four weeks of age, formula should be provided. The amount fed each day should be increased over a period of two weeks, when the puppies can be weaned completely. The formula should be prepared as described on page 41, warmed to lukewarm, and poured into a shallow pan placed on the floor of the box. After his mouth has been dipped into the mixture a few times, a puppy will usually start to lap formula. All puppies should be allowed to eat from the same pan, but be sure the small ones get their share. If they are pushed aside, feed them separately. Permit the puppies to nurse part of the time, but gradually increase the number of meals of formula. By the time the puppies are five weeks old, the dam should be allowed with them only at night. When they are about six weeks old, they should be weaned completely and fed the puppy diet described on page 41.

Once they are weaned, puppies should be given temporary distemper injections every two weeks until they are old enough for permanent inoculations. At six weeks, stool specimens should be checked for worms, for almost without exception, puppies become infested. Specimens should be checked again at eight weeks, and as often thereafter as your veterinarian recommends.

Sometimes owners decide as a matter of convenience to have a bitch spayed or a male castrated. While this is recommended when a dog has a serious inheritable defect or when abnormalities of reproductive organs develop, in sound, normal purebred dogs, spaying a bitch or castrating a male may prove a definite disadvantage. The operations automatically bar dogs from competing in shows as well as precluding use for breeding. The operations are seldom dangerous, but they should not be performed without good reason.